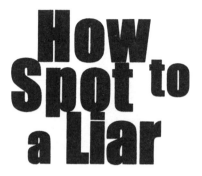

How Spot to a Liar

Why People
Don't Tell the *Truth*
...and How *You*
Can *Catch* Them

By
Gregory Hartley
and
Maryann Karinch

CASTLE
BOOKS

This edition published in 2007 by
CASTLE BOOKS ®
A division of Book Sales, Inc.
114 Northfield Avenue
Edison, NJ 08837

This edition published by arrangement with and permission of
The Career Press, Inc.
3 Tice Road
P.O. Box 687
Franklin Lakes, NJ 07417

How To Spot a Liar
Edited by Jodi Brandon

Library of Congress Cataloging-in-Publication Data:

Hartley, Gregory.
    How to spot a liar : why people don't tell the truth – and how you can catch them / Gregory Hartley and Maryann Karinch.
          p.   cm.
Includes index.
    1.   Truthfulness and falsehood – Psychological aspects.
    2.   Deception – Psychological aspects. I. Karinch, Maryann. II. Title.

BF637.T77H37 2005
155.9'2—dc22

2005050791

ISBN-13: 978-0-7858-2304-9
ISBN-10: 0-7858-2304-2

Printed in the United States of America

Dedication

To my grandmother Elsie Hartley for teaching me the difference between poor and low class.

—Greg

To Jim, mom, and Karl—I can always count on you for the truth.

—Maryann

Acknowledgments

I cannot thank Mike Ritz and Hollis Moore of Team Delta (teamdelta.net) enough for having the insight and vision to understand that interrogation is not confined to the interrogation room and for getting me in front of the national media. This book would not have occurred without Michael Dobson, who takes the blame for this collaboration since he prodded me to write and introduced me to Maryann. I am grateful to Allan Stein of Rutgers University School of Law for his assistance in understanding the jury selection process. Thank you to Dina for supporting me and keeping me sane with the added workload. I could not manage this without Jeffrey caring for the horses when we are both away. Thank you to Jim McCormick for his choice of words and his encouragement. Don Landrum has been an invaluable mentor over the years in making me the interrogator I became. Maryann, thank you for making this a painless and enjoyable process. Most importantly thanks to all men and women in uniform who protect us in anonymity on a daily basis.

—Greg Hartley

Thank you to Jim McCormick for keen insights, encouragement, and other practical support along the way. Great appreciation to Michael Dobson for introducing me to Greg as well as assisting us with ideas as our work developed and to Debbie Singer Dobson for generously contributing her expertise on personality profiles. A big thank you to Dean Hohl, who provided an engaging story and expertise on sorting styles. I am also grateful for the enthusiasm and support we have received from the Career Press team, specifically, Ron Fry, Mike Lewis, Kirsten Dalley, Kristen Parkes, Michael Pye, Jodi Brandon, Christopher Carolei, and Linda Reinecker. Thank you also to friends whose professions put them in a unique position to offer guidance on a book about truth-telling, especially Patti Mengers and Ray Decker. I also want to acknowledge experts whose research and writings laid the foundation for some of the insights in the book, including psychologist Paul Ekman and neurologist Antonio Damasio. And thank you, Greg, for being such a great partner!
—Maryann Karinch

Contents

Introduction

Why You Need This Book

Our bodies, including our brains, have remarkable similarities and striking differences. We have the same, fundamental physical structures—heart, mouth, neck, cerebral cortex, and so on. But I'm a lanky, red-headed male with big ears and beady eyes, and you're probably not. Add religion, culture, education, and other non-physical characteristics to the distinctions between us, and you and I seem even more dissimilar. Could it be true, then, that we broadcast the same signals when we tell lies or feel stress? No, and yes. It's not true that the eyes of all human beings wander off to the right when they're lying, but some of them do. It's not true that all people cross their arms when they don't want someone to invade their space, but some of them do. We can make a firm statement about only a few things, such as the fact that humans in a state of high anxiety smell really foul.

Zoologist Desmond Morris, author of classic works on behavioral links between people and our primitive ape ancestors, offered us a framework for documenting how we're *likely* to respond to certain stimuli. His conclusions should not be taken as absolutes, however, and that's why I can't offer you a simple checklist of ways to spot a liar. What I can do is teach you to determine on a case-by-case basis whether or not someone is lying—by what they are saying, or by what they're not telling you. I can also give you the steps to extracting the truth, as well as resisting efforts to make you divulge information you want to keep to yourself.

This book is a practical guide to learning and using the sophisticated psychological tools of interrogators. You need this book if someone has lied to you, manipulated you, or backed you into a corner. You need this book if you have an important relationship—with a spouse, boss, parent, client, child, employee, friend—that lacks honesty. You don't want to go through life wearing a sign that reads "victim" or "patsy." To make sure you don't, you need the techniques covered in this book that give you what I call "extreme interpersonal skills."

The book isn't just about managing your relationships with a cheating spouse or manipulative boss, however. The same techniques that help you turn those situations around are the ones that help you gain the upper hand in a salary negotiation, to draw a prospective client toward the outcome you design, and, in some cases, to find out why you need to end a business or personal relationship. They will help you conduct or succeed at job interviews and reel in prospective customers. Litigators who need to read character and establish truthfulness will find dozens of reliable ploys. Anyone who is trying to survive the dating scene, has teenagers at home, or works on Capitol Hill will find ways to cope and win.

People often ask me if I use these skills on my family and friends. The answer is, "No...as long as I have reasons to trust them."

—Greg Hartley

Section I:

Context

Chapter 1

Where Do These Techniques Come From?

(Or, What Does Abu Ghraib Have to Do With You?)

Why You Should Learn This

In daily life, I use the tools covered in this book when I don't trust someone or when I need to get the upper hand for a purpose. Using them constantly to manipulate loved ones and business associates would make me a sociopath. Using them wisely means that I understand I have entitlements—the right to humane treatment, honesty, fair play.

In your daily life, you have a range of choices about where you go and what you do; that allows you to operate with certainty. When I use the tools of interrogation, I create dilemmas so that prisoners have only two ugly options. They find themselves having to choose between doing something in their nature that they don't want to do, or doing something against their nature that they want to do. For example, truthful people divulge secrets even though it means betrayal of comrades, and loyal soldiers defect because they want to stop the bloodshed. In the first case, I force them to solve a problem by putting their needs over the needs of the group, and in the second, I push them to put the needs of the group over that of an individual. All I've done is exploit the human tendency to take the path of least resistance. This ability is an integral part of what you will learn.

Being an interrogator is a little similar to being a schoolyard bully: finding somebody's soft spots and pushing on them. That's why you have to be careful practicing the skills of an interrogator. Your life isn't war, so don't go around treating your kids and business associates as though they're enemy combatants you'll never see again. Your goai is to insist on honesty or detect stress so you can use it to get the result you want, not to manipulate those around you for sport.

Very few people know how to use the techniques described in this book—consciously, that is. Most of these skills exist in your repertoire, but you can't necessarily draw on them at will or use them in conjunction with related talents. Even most of the so-called interrogators who handle terrorist suspects at Guantanamo Bay are really questioners who do not have the training to influence human motivation, read body language, and orchestrate interrogation techniques. Asking good questions is one of the skills you're about to explore, but it's only one of many.

So, when you learn how to combine tactics of interrogation effectively—baseline, read body language, minimize, and so on—you will be unique. Unique because you bring a different set of experiences and traits to the game from me or anyone else who reads this book. When you understand the mechanics of stress and master the 12 basic approaches to manipulate someone's fears and dreams, you will be powerful. You may not be adept with these tools as soon as you put the book down, but give yourself time. This skill set grows over the years as does the human mind.

Why I Learned This

I started to develop interrogation skills in 1989 (and I'm still learning) with Army instruction that began with a desire to learn Arabic. Lots of Army interrogators, who are mostly enlisted personnel, want to learn a foreign language far more than they wanted to go head to head with prisoners. They are genuine romantics, and that's a big reason why most wash out. In fact, the attrition rate has been as high as 60 percent over the years. I, on the other hand, got excited when the Army told me I was going into a branch of the intelligence business. I found out that's now only a technical designation, though. Interrogators of the Cold War era, as did other Army intelligence officers, handled classified material behind a firewall that shielded them from the rest of the Army. In other words, interrogators did not have to see front-line action.

The U.S. intelligence machine in at-war mode, as it is now, is a large-scale prisoner collection operation with tiered prisoner-handling capacities. Prisoners wind their way from the front to collection sites and eventually to massive prisoner holding cages in the rear. These "cages" may be hundreds of miles from enemy activity and hold thousands of prisoners. Young soldiers with nothing more than a desire to use their language skills, limited training in psychology, and no capability to read body language, populate the process from front to rear. Mostly, these are in-language questioners; a talented few will become what I call an interrogator.

Interrogators need an operational knowledge to be effective; they can't function as other people in the Army intelligence business do. They need to know in a real way, not just a theoretical one, how enemy and friendly soldiers go about doing their job in order to ask questions that dig out essential facts.

In short, I needed to be put in harm's way in order to learn how to interrogate enemy soldiers who are forward-deployed. Fortunately, I was deployed with the 5th Special Forces Group to Operation Desert Storm. This taught me a valuable lesson that I'll pass along as you begin your "training": If you don't know what you're talking about, you put limits on what kind of information you'll be able to get. If you have ever been interviewed by a human resources screener who knew almost nothing about your skill set, you understand the limitation.

These techniques are not classified because they aren't taught. Approaches and questions fit into the curriculum for a military interrogator, but the sophisticated techniques of soft interrogation in the book come from years of practice, teaching, and independent study. Army interrogation school is a "10" level course, meaning it's entry level. There is no follow-on instruction. Think back to the most boring math or history course you ever took. This was just as dreary—day after day of questioning and reporting writing, practicing approaches in a sterile environment. Repeat *ad nauseam*. We got just enough skill to get in the face of the enemy and rattle him, hopefully with purpose and direction. And often the more advanced skills the Army does teach don't become practical tools for the young soldiers who use them. Their emotions and cognitive processes are still evolving rapidly, so how can we expect them to manage their own stress and thought patterns, much less someone else's? This makes the enemy prisoner-of-war cage in the rear all the more important to the way the U.S. Army conducts business: The young interrogator needs a safe place to practice.

From the Gulf War, I went to SERE school (Survival, Evasion, Resistance, Escape). There, I interrogated eight hours a day, three days a week, every other week for three and a half years—a total of 570 interrogations—to help our Special Forces learn how to resist interrogation. It was at SERE school that I met one of the most formative forces in my life, Don Landrum, well known as a founding member of Delta Force and of SERE. Don, *aka* "the

Bearded One," was not an interrogator, but he knew more about the tools and methods than I ever learned from the interrogation community. The particular expertise he taught me is the one I mentioned at the beginning of this chapter (how to pare a prisoner's sense of his options down to two: bad or worse).

When the first Gulf War started, I was assigned to the Special Warfare Center at Ft. Bragg. There were only 55 Arabic-speaking interrogators in the entire U.S. Army, and we had six of them. In my class, just two of us spoke Arabic; everyone else spoke Russian, Czech, Polish—the languages of people who were America's Cold War enemies. This is one reason why I got so much experience and contact with Iraqi soldiers. When I was handpicked for the 5th Special Forces Group, my initial assignment took me to a team supporting the Saudi Arabian Army. Shortly thereafter, I began working with a team supporting the Kuwaiti brigade. I screened more than 100 enemy prisoners during Operation Desert Storm and interrogated a couple of dozen of them.

During this period is when I really learned how to read body language and first discovered how to teach the techniques of interrogations. I also began to see the analogous relationship between using them in war and applying them in my daily life. By the way, just because I know these things does not mean I'm impervious to emotional outbursts or that I intimidate my friends by "reading" them and using words to back them into a corner. I do have a greater awareness of my emotions, however, and when my friends have stress in their lives, I'll probably notice it before other people would. I also have substantially more power than other people in most business situations, and arguments with the woman I love tend to be sane and productive instead of crazy and misdirected.

Interrogation History

Where does interrogation come from? As a science, it's relatively new, but people have interrogated prisoners forever. Roman soldiers wanted to know where their comrades were being held by locals during an invasion. Soldiers would pull captured enemies and torture them to get information, but there was no system. Even in the Civil War, we didn't have a method for interrogating prisoners. We thought of them simply as combatants removed from the battle field. We kept prisoners in massive compounds as if they were cattle in a pen, doing nothing more than keeping troops out of combat. Eight thousand people died of cholera in Andersonville, Georgia, where the national POW monument now stands. The Elmira, New York, compound, known as Hellmira in the Civil War, had comparable tragic deaths resulting from abuse and neglect. Jump ahead to World War II and the time from a commander's decision to troop movement and weapons deployment accelerated so rapidly that the value of interrogating prisoners could not be overlooked. Prisoners suddenly had value alive. But the United States was among the many countries that lacked a specially trained interrogation force.

Modern war operations are predictive on a scale unlike anything in history. So interrogators who grew up in this modern era found themselves trying to be like Superman: to hear conversations that went on far away, to see through walls into strange buildings. Where the analogy melts is in verifying the information. Superman personally hears and sees, whereas interrogators have to rely on what someone else has seen or heard. What they learn can therefore be information or disinformation.

The only way to do this was to understand the psychology of why people talk, when they talk, and how they talk. To know whether they lie or tell the truth, how to tell when they're lying, how to tell when they're telling the truth. These needs drove the development of the science of interrogation, which must have the aura of "witchcraft." That is, as a layperson you can't figure out why it works, but it does.

Interrogators had a bad reputation for a while, too, just as the witches at Salem did. That has shifted over the past few decades when the concept of collecting intelligence directly from human sources has gained respect. During the Cold War, people who interpreted radio signals and satellite imagery surpassed interrogators in their value to military operations. These people used equipment worth millions of dollars. It was more cost-effective and covert to use technology to collect strategic and tactical information than it was to nab scientists and political officials and interrogate them. By the time of the first Gulf War, however, something approaching 85 percent of intelligence came from human sources. One reason: Saddam Hussein relied on couriers more than electronic means. The idea of a Cold War enemy with advanced technology and a sophisticated communications net dissolved when dealing with developing nations. Add to this the complexity of our modern war on terror and clandestine communications, and you can see why an interrogator is in high demand today.

You Are a Prisoner

Here's where I really begin to answer the question in the chapter subtitle: "What Does Abu Ghraib Have to Do With You?"

Fundamentally, the tools of interrogation that I've used with prisoners have value in your everyday life because you have a lot in common with a prisoner of war. First and foremost, you both have a little black box inside you that makes you who you are, and there are many forces at work that could potentially destroy what's inside it. Second, the stress of being captured and then being a captive has corollary in your daily life.

You've no doubt heard at least one story of a hard-charging soldier who died at enemy hands because he refused to talk. For him the most sacred part of himself, that little box inside that contained his core identity, was the duty to protect others' lives by protecting certain information. Another soldier, just as devoted to duty, might crack under pressure and violate that sacred part of himself. He might still be alive, but he is no longer alive as the same person.

Everyone has a little box. You may not even know what it contains, but if you lose it, you face a kind of personal extinction. Essentially, you become a stranger to yourself when you ravage a core belief or value, or when someone else manipulates you toward the same end. On a regular basis—just as a captured soldier does—you face situations like that, as well as individuals who have the potential to cause that destruction.

Shock of Capture (or, Turning Your Toy Box Upside Down)

When a person is captured, his stress levels go through the roof. If capture comes after a firefight, he knows many of his friends have just died, which adds emotions such as grief and anger to the fear that runs through his entire body. This is the most dangerous moment in that person's life. Adrenaline levels are high; conscious thought isn't. I, the enemy, have just killed people he cares about, so his pores ooze hatred for me, my comrades, my commander, my country. He has just as much terror about what I might do to him.

Another scenario has him on patrol; we abduct him quickly with no one getting killed. Capture never feels good, so his hostility will rise. Suddenly, he becomes truly helpless because his captors are screaming orders—"You #$%^, get on the ground! Put your hands behind your head!" He's like a dog, who only hears, "Blah, blah, blah! Blah blah, blah!" The tone of voice is clear, but the directions aren't. If he does the wrong thing, will he die? That's possible, and he knows it. Anxiety, a by-product of fear of the unknown, shuts down the thinking brain and turns on the body-protecting, or reacting, brain. Interrogators are brokers of anxiety. It is the product we sell.

In a recent taping for British TV, our group, composed of people associated with Team Delta, a school founded by one of my former students, abducted seven volunteers at breakfast—not when they expected it. Our participants included Britain's fittest fireman. Adam is a bright, engaging man who is accustomed to stress. His response to capture is demonstrated on the video when he is told by multiple people to look right, look at me, look left. The orders obviously confuse him. Finally, he hears, "Look down," at which point he gets to his knees. Adam is trying to predict what we want so hard that he projects what we want. This is a man accustomed to high stress with English-speaking captors. Imagine the stress when your captors speak a foreign language and you are an 18-year-old conscript.

What are his psychological defenses in either situation? He brings his wealth of experiences, or dearth of them, and his identities to the situation. He is a soldier, husband, son, and guitarist in a garage band. Nowhere in that spectrum of defining roles is he a captive, so he has to learn to be a captive rather than draw from memory. Human brains function well when they have areas to store information, and they falter when information invades and has no place to go. Every time we experience something new, we build a mailbox in our head for related, future knowledge and experience. This makes it much harder to suffer displaced expectation in the future.

Think of the collapse of the World Trade Center's Twin Towers. You might have been able to envision a plane crashing into a building, but could you absorb the magnitude of what happened on September 11, 2001? That sight shocked me, as it did millions of people. Our minds did not include a box for that information; it overwhelmed us. The first time you saw a dead body or rear-ended a car you probably had the same reaction, just to a different degree.

The captive, therefore, confronts the dual trauma of direct exposure to the enemy and a new, overwhelming experience. Notable exceptions would be people such as the Special Forces troops that we trained in SERE school. Building on the premise that the more you become accustomed to an experience, the more you are able to cope with it, we subjected those soldiers to hundreds of capture scenarios. In wartime, they have "only" the trauma of exposure to the enemy and his alien horrors.

You can understand, therefore, why a captured frontline infantry soldier would suffer more confusion and shock than an intelligence officer. His frame of reference is different; he goes into the situation with a profound disadvantage, unprepared for a particular kind of enemy assault. He probably doesn't speak the language of the enemy, has just been busy shooting his captor's friends, and instantly plummets from being a powerful guy with a gun to someone subdued, cuffed, and at the mercy of a man with a gun. The moment he experiences such displaced expectations—not having a box in his head to place and process what's happened to him—he is extremely vulnerable.

The essence of this man comes from a complex interplay of connections in his daily life. "Self" embodies input from others and from situations. "Frame of reference," or a picture of the outside world, is prejudiced by experiences. This man has just suffered a severe blow to both self and frame of reference. No longer the rifle-carrying soldier, he is now the helpless captive who failed his mission. All of his defined traits for that role begin to fill his head. Most of these definitions are negative and have been driven into him by military superiors and movies. He's now a loser, and the captor won't play the role of counselor unless it fits the captor's needs.

Effects of Captivity

The *shock of capture* seems to be the worst thing that will ever happen to the prisoner at the moment it occurs, but there is more. After the initial terror and fear for his life, the prisoner starts to adapt. He gets a mailbox in his head to help him cope with the stress. Prisoners sometimes even feel cavalier and try to make demands. Most prisoners are segregated and silenced so there is no opportunity to console or collaborate. The prisoner is left alone with his need to talk about failure and feelings of inadequacy. In many cases the prisoner is blindfolded and cuffed to allow the limited number of captors or escorts to manage him and his comrades safely. The deprivation of sight, though important for controlling an enemy combatant, creates the need for a guard or captor to become the eyes and guide for the prisoner. This begins a cycle of dependence that will only get worse as captivity progresses. When the prisoner encounters his first interrogator it will be in the form of a screener. Screeners have one purpose, which is to answer these two questions: Can this guy answer my requirements? and How hard is it going to be to get him to talk? There is something obviously different about the interrogator from the moment the prisoner meets him: He speaks the language. The cycle of dependence is becoming more entrenched.

The interrogator may or may not be interested in the prisoner. The guards are interested only in safety and control. Their job is to follow a clearly defined doctrine on how to handle the prisoner. The result is a dance. The guard gives input to the prisoner and the prisoner responds. The guard uses this stimulus of the prisoner's response to flesh out his newly found role as all powerful caretaker. The guard responds with whatever tools are in his repertoire and the prisoner takes this input to help define his new role as prisoner. New prisoners and new guards continually create steps for their dance. Without diligent supervision, the guard and prisoner can become unwitting participants in a field version of "the Stanford prison experiment," that disastrous 1971 exercise in which middle-class kids assumed the roles of guards and prisoners.

When the prisoner encounters someone who speaks his language there is a natural affinity. He's desperately in need of companionship. Humans are social creatures and need re-inforcement. The self-portrait the prisoner had has now become blurred. The picture has voids for the roles he filled in his unit as a soldier. The newfound role of prisoner takes him off balance. The prisoner gets into a cycle of dependence that resembles regression, or drops back to the last time in his life that someone made all decisions for him. The prisoner becomes wholly dependent on the guards and interrogators to tell him what the correct answer to every question is. If shock of capture turned the toy box upside down, this can be likened to moving the playground.

All of the details that have been validated in the past about the prisoner's intelligence and good looks now need nurturing. There is no source for this data. The prisoner begins an internal conversation, one aimed at regaining equilibrium. In this conversation, the prisoner is the standard, so any self doubt becomes magnified. If the prisoner has a fault or failure it becomes the primary focus. If he and four others were captured by 250 enemy soldiers, the internal dialogue centers on which of the four is to blame. The prisoner personalizes everything that happens, and the welfare of others becomes less important. Any threat to health in the compound is only perceived in terms of how it can injure him.

The stress that was the shock of capture takes on new meaning when interrogations begin. Being captured and removed from the battlefield removes a warrior from the random haphazard attacks of the battlefield and into a battlefield that is personalized and designed for one-on-one combat. These feelings of inadequacy will be preyed upon. Whether the interrogator compounds or allays these feelings is dictated by the psychological makeup of the prisoner.

Pandering to the captor to keep him happy results in *Stockholm Syndrome*. The prisoner starts to identify with the captor and even emulate behaviors and speech patterns. Stockholm Syndrome can occur in a few days.

What does this have to do with you? You aren't behind bars in an orange jumpsuit. You eat good food, not stale rations. You walk about freely and bathe daily. But you're in a kind of captivity. You wake up and wonder why you'll get yelled at today. You look out the window and dream of running away—from school, from home, from your job. You choke on each meal that you have with someone who has locked you up emotionally. Captivity. You answer the phone and are too polite to hang up on a fundraiser. Rather than have to say "no," you make a promise you can't keep.

Clearly, you do understand captivity to some degree if you live in this civilized society. We are trapped by things our parents teach us. We are trapped by society's rules.

We are trapped by everything we know. For example, Mormons are typically very trusting people, so many Utah communities passed stringent laws against door-to-door solicitation to protect them from exploitation. Utah legislators didn't want their neighbors "trapped" in their homes. When a telemarketer keeps you on the phone for any length of time, he's preying on your manners. It's not any different from what interrogators do when they use cultural norms against an enemy combatant.

A variation on this is how interrogators at a compound such as Guantanamo Bay might manipulate societal norms on a daily basis to create a system of *displaced expectations*. This process may sound familiar to anyone familiar with the situation of a battered spouse. In the case of the prisoner, he might think that behaving in a certain way will buy him some relief from questioning or earn him a piece of favorite food because that's what happened on Monday. On Tuesday, that same behavior will lead to endless push-ups or name-calling. How is that substantively different from the woman who lives in fear every day because nothing she does seems to please her husband? He makes the rules and, try as she may, she can't figure out what they are from day to day, so she "earns" a beating.

I could look at lots more parallels between military and civilian situations in which interrogation tools cause or relieve stress, but the basic point is this: Stress is stress is stress. An altercation with an employer, a fight in a bar, an argument with your lover—your mind can't tell the difference between that and gunfire. In mechanical terms, you are dealing with responses linked to self-preservation. When the conditions of captivity, as I described them here, are the same as those of a prisoner of war, your response is the same as a prisoner of war.

Go a step further. Any conditions that create unease, restlessness, instability, and/or unpredictability give you experiences in common with a prisoner of war. What if you came back from vacation and found that someone had rearranged your office, moved the coffeemaker, and put in a new phone system? You experience a temporary loss of control that may overwhelm you. You lose your ability to function at your peak because you move out of cognitive thought and into an emotional state, or *limbic mode*.

You Are an Animal

Are you a primate, a lower mammal, or a reptile?

In *The Owner's Manual for the Brain: Everyday Applications from Mind-Brain Research* (Bard Press, 1999), Pierce J. Howard discusses the three brains:

> . . . the lizard brain was simply geared only to the maintenance of survival functions: respiration, digestion, circulation, and reproduction.... Extending out of the lizard brain stem, the leopard brain (now called the limbic system) added to the animal's behavioral repertoire the capacity for emotion and coordination of movement. This second phase of brain evolution yielded the well known General Adaptation Syndrome (GAS), or fight or flight response. The third phase of evolution was the learning brain—the cerebral cortex. This third and most recent phase of brain evolution provided the ability to solve problems, use language and numbers, develop memory, and be creative. (pp. 37–39)

I interpret Howard's categories as reptilian, mammalian, and primate.

When you use your cerebral cortex for language, calculations, and other logical functions, you are a primate. Your limbic system, which enables you to experience and express emotion, belongs to your mammalian self. And the reptilian brain cares only about the basics: hunger, sex, survival.

As a person's stress level rises—even without touching or screaming—hormone production increases. It's the onset of the cortisol cycle. In short, two small glands near the kidneys called the adrenals, or "stress glands," kick in. We couldn't survive stress without them because they fuel us for fight, which can be verbal or physical, or to escape the danger.

The human peripheral nervous system contains two components for regulating conscious mind: sympathetic and parasympathetic. The sympathetic agitates the body and prepares the human for fight or flight; the parasympathetic is responsible for resting and relaxing the human body. See these as a sort of upper and downer set of controls for the human mind.

High Stress and the Sympathetic Nervous System

The sympathetic system engages in response to a perceived threat within milliseconds of the initial shock that triggers the cortisol cycle. Everything that the stress hormones—cortisol, DHEA, and adrenaline—are going to do to your body to prepare it for fight or flight happens in that sliver of time. The body, not the mind, decides which systems are needed for the perceived threat. These systems turn on at the cost of others not deemed necessary. In rapid fire, the body takes these actions:

*   Routes blood away from the face and skin and to the muscles.

- Diverts blood away from the digestive and reproductive systems.
- Loses the capability to contract the bladder and expel waste.
- Floods with glucose from the liver to prepare for physical activity.
- Sends blood to the reptilian and mammalian brains at the expense of the primate brain.
- Raises heart action in order to get this blood to all the right places.
- Increases respiration in response to the heart pushing glucose through the systems, fucling the muscles with oxygen.
- Heightens metabolic requirements, so the body starts to sweat.
- Dilates pupils to collect data about the threat.

This is your mind at war.

There are inward and outward signs of this activity. Inwardly, the signs are the jittery, hypersensitive feeling signaling you are poised for action. Due to the lack of blood to the digestive system, you may get butterflies or a sick feeling. Your heart races with blood leaving the skin so you get the feeling of a high core temperature and cool skin (that is, you feel clammy). Your breathing is elevated, but constricted, so your heart and lungs race. This increased metabolism—as much as 100 percent—results in you feeling flushed and hot. Your focus becomes narrow and your hearing directed to the target. You can hear your heartbeat. Your mind recedes into the primitive state and emotions come to the fore. This explains why so many people cry when confronted and angry. Don't perceive this as weak or fragile.

Outwardly, there are noticeable signs as well:

- The body's decision to take blood from the skin results in a pallid complexion.
- Being part of the digestive system, the mucosa of the lips and mouth have dramatically reduced blood flow; lips and other mucosa shrink, resulting in pale thin lips and drooping lower eye lids.
- The increased heart rate may show in the pounding of the chest or rise and fall of the shoulders.
- Hands may shake in response to increased metabolism.
- Increased need for air results in flared nostrils and audible breathing.
- The eyes have focused on the cause of the stress and this can result in a squint or wide-open eyes, depending on the situation.
- The brow clinches and draws downward. Lips tighten to a thin colorless line.
- Shoulders draw higher in preparation for defense or escape.
- The body's increased need for glucose can start to scavenge from the mucosa and leave white residue in the corners of the mouth.
- Elbows go close to the ribs.
- Palms turn down and the hands close to form fists. In extreme terror this can go even further, resulting in the elbows drawing to the ribs and the hands moving to protect the face, in a reflexive effort to protect the area around the vital organs—oddly enough, leaving the top of the head unprotected.

- The increased need for cooling causes the body to sweat, and in this sweat are massive amounts of by-products; the fight-or-flight body odor is noticeable.
- Ultimately, the person collapses.

These are the effects of the sympathetic nervous system forcing us into man's most primitive reaction: fight or flight. At this point most of us function more similar to the leopard or other mammal than a human. We operate in limbic mode and only limbic memories are truly available for processing.

It's not a joke that dogs can smell fear, by the way. The body generates a complex odor—sticky sweet, metallic, bitter—from the kind of particle breakdown triggered by high stress. When I first got into this line of work, I used to think that the smell related to hygiene and diet. We'd send soldiers into the woods for eight days with no toilet paper or toothbrush and very little food. I figured the stink came from lack of washing and from ketosis, a process in which the body robs proteins and fats to make up for a carbohydrate deficit. Ketosis plays a role in the odor, but isn't triggered by bad diet. Stress makes the metabolic system ramp up and starts attacking proteins in the mouth and other areas where the material is easiest to break down. The result is that sickly smell—you can even taste it—that we call "prisoner funk." I've worked with prisoners and trainees from the United States, the Middle East—all over the world. Regardless of diet, the smell is remarkably similar from person to person. Now that you're aware of it, you would recognize it immediately. It's so thick, a single washing won't even take it out of your clothes.

The most serious symptom of high stress is collapse. First, the subject goes pale and has to go to the bathroom.

Next, the body runs out of adrenaline, and cortisol enters the picture. Cortisol regulates blood pressure and cardiovascular function. If the adrenal glands madly secrete it, the person will eventually collapse into a fetal position and go into shock.

Practicing a sport or fight sequence under stress can make up for the fact that cognitive abilities are gone when high performance is needed most. This is why martial artists, for example, practice moves with the aggression and sounds associated with battle: When the time comes, their bodies automatically know what to do. This applies to any athlete who competes seriously. Simulating the stress conditions of competition in addition to practicing specific moves prepares them to succeed even when their ability to think is diminished.

As the cortisol cycle continues, your brain regresses from primate to mammalian to reptilian. It dehumanizes, starting at a minimal level and moving all the way to reducing you to nothing but the basest cravings.

So here is one more way of answering the question, "What does Abu Ghraib have to do with you?" Prisoners under stress lose their ability to function logically, and so do you. They also leak emotions, just as you do.

In *The Feeling of What Happens* (Harcourt, 1999), neurologist Antonio Damasio points out the difference between "feeling" and "knowing that we have a feeling." He suggests, that, by the time we know we have a feeling, it's too late to do anything about it (p. 26). The body has already started giving responses to the emotions, whether they are primary ones such as surprise, or secondary emotions— Damasio calls them "social emotions"—such as guilt. He also cites the telltale signs of "background emotions," which include states such as calm, a general feeling of well-being, and tension:

. . . overall body posture and the range of motion of the limbs relative to the trunk; the spatial profile of limb movements, which can be smooth or jerky; the speed of motions; the congruence of movements occurring in different body tiers such as face, hands, and legs; and last and perhaps most important, the animation of the face. (p. 92)

Damasio's categories of behaviors that we all share point out where to look for the differences in the way people express stress. Just how "smooth or jerky" you move your arms, or how you twist your face into a disgusted look add variations to basic patterns. Add to that the genetics, culture, training, and so on that go into making each of us unique and it becomes impossible to be certain what specific body responses mean—with two exceptions. The first exception is, if you know what a person does with her arms, hands, legs, and face under normal circumstances (the baseline), then you can spot deviations. As long as you know what to look for—and this is a big part of what I'm going to share with you in this book—those deviations can tell you for certain that she's under stress. The second exception is a human being's range of reactions to very high stress.

You can't do much to counter or cover up flashing pupils, flaring nostrils, dilated facial pores, and sagging facial muscles—all the result of intense stress. You can easily see why people get unattractive when they're under stress for a long time. The condition of the skin condition deteriorates, facial muscles lose their tone, lips get thin— not a good time for the prom. On the other hand, when someone is charged up sexually, blood flow increases to the mucosa. Lips get thicker, the salivary glands gear up, and the entire face takes on a softer look. You're more sexually appealing, and your arousal is obvious. I've tried to explain this many times to my friends who complain that they can never tell if a person is attracted to them.

Recovery and the Parasympathetic Nervous System

After the sympathetic dumps adrenaline into your system and reduces you to the mental state of a lizard, the parasympathetic introducing other hormones which level out your system.

The parasympathetic brings your body back to a state of relaxation. Systems that were turned off begin to function again. The body decides to allow those "unnecessary" systems such as reproduction, digestion, and waste removal to function again. Your body is now akin to a war zone after the war: It's clean-up time. You start to think rationally as blood returns to the primate brain. You realize that the result of that super-charged metabolism and overly active kidneys and adrenal cortex have filled your bladder to a much higher degree than normal. You now have the capacity to contract your bladder as well as the urge to do so. All of the activities that you took for granted begin to return and you realize that your mouth is dry; you want a drink. The results of the adrenaline and heightened glucose leave your hands shaking; you become cognizant of this. Blood returns to your skin. Your face flushes and you feel warm. As the primate brain gets back to normal you start to realize that you were out of control. This preys on your need to conform to social norms and you feel guilty. In the truest of human fashion you are a social animal and you need to communicate.

As the interrogator, I see that and take advantage of it. I am here to help.

You've probably heard that someone red in the face is the most dangerous. Not true. Pale is more dangerous.

A pale person is in fight-or-flight mode. His lips are thin because all of the blood's gone from his mucous membranes, his muscles are pumped, and he is ready to fight. When the parasympathetic nervous system kicks in, blood returns to the face.

Exercise

Dress oddly, and then go a shopping mall or a well-trafficked city street, and walk around. I don't mean wear a costume. I mean wear clothes that reflect bad taste—so bad that you don't feel comfortable appearing in public in them. When people look at you out of pity, curiosity, or amusement, take note of how you feel. Notice how your stress level shifts in response to others' reactions to you.

You Are an Interrogator

I began this chapter by asserting that you have interrogation skills in your repertoire, but that you probably don't use them consciously or in concert with one another. I'll give you a couple of examples of why this is a fact, so you can move ahead with the confidence that you're building on abilities, not learning entirely new ones.

You routinely screen people to get various types of information from them—that is, you match your question to both your source and your specific need for information. What you probably don't do is evaluate information in terms of its strategic, tactical or quick-fix role. In other words, is it important for your big picture? Steps toward achieving some goal? Or does the information just fill an immediate need, such as tell you where the bathroom is?

When I was forward-deployed, I would interrogate recently captured soldiers. I'd go after low-ranking guys and had minutes to find out the key bits of information at that moment, such as "What else is dangerous to us here?" Strategic information about battle plans couldn't be my focus, although I'd certainly put any indication that a prisoner had that knowledge in my report so someone could dig for it after we found out where the land mines and snipers were.

A low-ranking soldier, generally the easiest to milk, represented a source of this tactical "level-C" information to me. In business, the analogous person is the receptionist. When you enter a prospect's offices, you connect with the person at the front desk and pick up tidbits about the company. Your level-C information doesn't give you weighty insights about the executive you'll be meeting, which would be level-B or -A information, but it does give you details that could help give you connect better with the executive or maybe even get leverage with him or her.

You routinely establish rapport with co-workers, prospective mates, and other new acquaintances. In doing so, you unknowingly use the same tools an interrogator uses. You ask questions about subjects you have no interest in— non-pertinent questions in the parlance of interrogation— to get the conversation started. The answers can also give you a feel for the person's likes, dislikes, rate of speech, mannerisms, and cadence. It's natural to reflect some of that back to the person; this is a form of mirroring.

Desmond Morris points out in *Manwatching: A Field Guide to Human Behavior* (Harry N. Abrams, 1979) that all people in all cultures will begin to adopt the body language of others in their small groups. Mirroring is a natural way to show a connection with the person with whom you're talking. I watched two young people out on a date recently who were clearly too young to have been out on too many dates. The boy would lean into the table to talk, as if telling the girl a secret. The girl would respond in kind and then tilt her head to match his. No one taught them these signals of interest, respect, flirting, or however you would categorize them.

You can consciously mirror, too, to convey those positive feelings and raise the other person's comfort level. As long as it doesn't look contrived, it advances the process of getting them to talk.

Questioning is natural for humans, too. It has been said that what makes us humans is the desire to explore. Who cannot remember a child asking "why?" When I heard Arab children in Kuwait doing the same thing, I realized it's probably a trait that little kids have in common all over the world. Many of us never outgrow it. Our curiosity constantly surfaces in the form of questions. The difference between that natural, spontaneous questioning and interrogation is the clarity of the questions. Interrogators design their questions in advance for a specific purpose.

You Are a Lie Detector

You will probably be a little mechanical when you first try out the techniques I'm teaching. After a while, though, you'll find yourself sensitized to the signals of deception and stress; your new skills will be second nature. You'll become a lie detector. And then, when people around you fall for the charisma of a devious politician, for example, you'll be able to give them solid reasons why the person has no business tampering with your democracy. The techniques of interrogation can help you distance yourself from fuzzy auras such as "charisma" and ask critical questions that spotlight deception, or at least reveal inconsistencies. Even on a non-verbal level, you will pick up that a person is too slick, is too glossy, and is therefore hiding something. Little bells will go off in your head that signal "Lie. Lie. Lie." And people will pay attention to you because they'll know you're telling the truth.

Chapter 2

Why and How People Lie

Why You Lie

People lie out of love, hate, or greed. Self-preservation is a form of self love that ranks at the top of the list of reasons why people lie. Usually, it's not literal self-preservation, but perceived. For example, you come home after a night of hard partying and your wife, who's just put infant twins to bed, says, "Where've you been?!" You could be honest and reply, "Doing tequila shooters at a strip bar with my brother." Or you could sidestep the truth by saying, "My brother and I got together after work to have a drink and talk about his job. He's really unhappy." On the other hand, a killer on trial for first-degree murder has the challenge of literal self-preservation: He lies to save himself from execution. In a real interrogation, self-preservation takes on a different dimension. A soldier who lies skillfully can protect not only his life, but also the lives of comrades.

Military interrogators don't care if their target is guilty or innocent, by the way. They want to stop something from happening, so they want information. Genuine expressions of sorrow, grief, or guilt mean only one thing: weakness that makes the desired information more accessible. As an interrogator, therefore, I'm not judgmental. I could talk with Charles Manson as easily as the ice cream man. I'm more interested in how his brain works than in judging him. You may find that one of the side effects of practicing these techniques is that you develop a similar inclination to look for the facts rather than the "right" or "wrong." To paraphrase a biblical lesson, one result might be that you will be more able to hate the sin but love the sinner. When people observe this trait in you, they will probably be more willing to tell you the truth.

Although it's easy to understand self-preservation as a motive for lying, it assumes a level of complexity when the liar lies to everyone. Usually, there's a friend, confidante, priest, or therapist with whom the liar would be honest. But sometimes, the scenario is devoid of honesty.

Lie to wife: "I'm not having an affair."

Lie to girlfriend: "I plan to marry you."

Lie to friends: "I would never cheat on my wife."

Why would an individual such as this, who's having an affair, lie to everyone? There are three possibilities:

- He can't tell the truth, meaning he's a sociopath.
- He's so ashamed that the truth hurts no matter who hears it.
- He has something to hide that no one can know about.

A second reason to lie is to be polite, which again can be a form of love. "Honey, do these pants make my butt look big?" invites a wisecrack such as, "No. But your butt sure makes those pants look small." Most people would probably agree that it's more polite to say something farther from the truth: "No."

Sometimes, it's just easier to lie than it is to tell the truth. Again, this could be a form of self-love. When people who don't know my friend Kay very well ask how her husband died, she might say simply, "He was sick for a long time." She invites pity, confusion, and painful questions if she spills the facts: "He died of a self-inflicted gunshot wound to the head."

Another love-based lie might be to protect someone else. It's the case of the little boy who takes the blame for breaking a window to protect his friend from getting beaten by a cruel dad.

A lie rooted in hate could involve a country, ideology, person—all the same categories that a lie of love involves. A soldier will lie to help destroy an enemy. A business executive might lie to damage a competitor. I know of a woman who lied about her estranged husband molesting their children. She wanted him out of her and her children's lives so desperately that she fabricated his abusive behavior.

Finally, people lie for personal gain, or greed. Exaggerations on a resumé, inflated deductions on a tax return, and glossy stories of your days as a college athlete—all are lies that "everybody" tells.

If you have children, I'll put money on the fact that you taught them to lie. From "tell him I'm not home" when you get a call from someone you want to avoid to "tell Great Aunt Hazel how nice she looks" when she shows up for dinner wearing two different shoes, you condition your children to lie to be polite, for self-preservation, and so on. You don't want your 6-year-old to blurt out in the grocery store, "But, mom, I couldn't reach the cereal because that fat woman was standing in front of it."

There are also times when an untruth is not a lie. Two different people can remember different details of the same event to such a great extent that their stories contradict each other. Eyewitnesses to a crime can be unreliable sources of information because of the combination of stress, point of view, influences from other eyewitnesses, and so on. No one is lying, but no one is telling the truth. And, yes, men and women have slightly different brains so they may have conflicting versions of the same story—with neither one being wrong or deceptive.

Shadowy memories can involve a kind of lie as well. If you aren't trained to think under stress and, for example, you're raped or captured, your brain has the capacity to create shadowy memories. The limbic system transfers information into memory—that's normal—but, if that happens in a highly emotional state, then the way you recall the memory could happen in unpredictable ways. A climate change or odor that reminds a rape victim of the event might elicit a shadowy memory, the details of which could be profoundly affected by feelings. A shadowy memory isn't necessarily bad, however. The temperature of the air could remind you of your first skydive and lead to a story that isn't exactly built out of facts, but, to you, that's the way it was.

Regardless of why you lie, the lie itself causes stress. It doesn't matter if your motivation is thoroughly decent, such as a lie to protect your family from harm. There is an incompatibility between what you're doing and what your brain is telling you to do.

The Mechanics of Lying

People tell lies in four basic ways: They omit, commit, embellish the truth, and transfer.

- Why did you start your own business? "I felt stifled working for such a big company, so I took my good ideas and struck out on my own." You omit the part about being fired.
- Why did you start your own business? "Customers told me I was the reason they were so

loyal to the company and they'd rather deal with me directly." Hogwash. An even more common style of lying by "commission," or pure fabrication, is through a simple denial or affirmation: Did you finance your new business with your own money? You say "yes" even though the money came from your husband's trust fund.

◆ Why did you start your own business? "I had the best sales record in the company and knew I could succeed on my own." True, except that 19 people shared "the best sales record in the company."

◆ Why did you start your own business? "My research showed that a community like this really needs the service." Actually, it was your friend's research about his community, which is a lot like yours. Transference simply means you take a slice of someone else's truth and make it your own. It's a tough lie to defend because you're pulling a story out of context. Making up the details can be rough unless you know the other person's life extremely well.

My friend dated a successful salesman who commonly lied through transference. After a few months, she called him on it and he'd laugh and tell her to lighten up. He viewed his lying as a kind of party trick—pure entertainment. One evening in the company of some people he'd never met before, he described a battle he'd supposedly been part of in Vietnam. People asked questions focused directly on the story, so he got away with his vivid descriptions woven out of the details of someone else's life. Two types of questions could have easily tripped him up: something that plunged him into another context related to the story, or something involving pure conjecture that was related to the story. For example, "What was your basic training like?" is something the liar would have trouble answering if he'd never been in the military. And a question involving speculation—"What do you think would have happened if the Viet Cong troops had seen you?" for example—could cause him to trail off, change the subject, or make up something ridiculous on the fly. And if you're studying his face and body for signs of lying, you might notice that, instead of signaling that he's thinking creatively, he's actually accessing a memory. That's a sure sign that whatever he says next is part of a rehearsed story.

Cover stories come apart, which is why trained soldiers rarely use lies of transference or of commission. It is too easy to break the liar by questioning details. Legendary German interrogator Hans Scharff demonstrated this time after time. Scharff developed *soft interrogation* techniques to earn prisoners' trust that often succeeded because of his attention to details. For example, he had personally travelled extensively in Europe and knew train schedules, distances, and other details that he ultimately used to shred the stories of captured Allied soldiers. For this reason, I've always taught my interrogation students that there are no useless bits of information.

You will simplify your life enormously if you eliminate complete fabrication from your repertoire. It's relatively easy to spot, as you will soon see, and very tough to defend with credible details. I'm going to teach you to read body language that will help you tear that kind of liar apart. But in Chapter 14, on self-defense, I will also give you steps to turning the details of a lie into "truth" in your head—tricks of the pros, such as field operatives for intelligence agencies and undercover cops.

I would not advocate total elimination of omission and embellishment. These brands of lying are a fact of life that help human beings deal with myriad challenges. It's better than letting your mouth say whatever your brain thinks. That's what children do before they learn social skills. They have no filter, no private thoughts. Habitually engaging in a childlike "radical honesty," a concept described by Brad Blanton in a book of the same name (Dell, 1996), will hurt people—for what reason?—and alienate even close friends.

Do take a hard look at why you want to lie by omission or embellishment, though. Both can strain relationships to the breaking point if they violate expectations, or *entitlements*. Fidelity is a common entitlement, even if the couple doesn't have a marriage contract that specifies it. A woman asking her fiancé, "Did you see your ex-girlfriend when you were in San Antonio?" most likely doesn't want a "yes" or "no." She expects you to know that the word "see" really means "have sexual contact with," so your answer better be complete enough to address that question. When you say "yes" and leave it at that, it can be a fact that sounds deceitful! The elephant is in the living room and no one wants to admit it.

Exercise

As you watch television or a video one evening, make a list of the types of lies the characters introduce (self-preservation, polite, and so forth). How did the type of lie affect your perception of the character? How did it affect the character(s) who was told the lie?

The Styles of Lying

In the early 1970s Richard Bandler and John Grinder conducted research at the University of California that led to neurolinguistic programming (NLP). It's valuable in understanding how people absorb and sort information, and, as a corollary, how they lie. A key concept in NLP is that the ability to establish rapport with others supersedes natural intelligence and formal education in helping a person achieve success. You can define success broadly as in "a successful life" or you can narrow it down to "a successful cold call" or "successfully cheating on your spouse." But the core concept here is "rapport." To establish rapport you have to use the most ideal information channel for the individual. Next, you need to adapt to the way a person sorts information.

So how a person lies, or really how well a person lies, depends on these rapport skills. How well a person interrogates also depends on these rapport skills.

Access Senses

The primary information channels, or access senses, are visual, auditory, and kinesthetic. Most people respond to visual stimuli more keenly than the others, but there are people for whom hearing or feeling something leaves a stronger impression. In the next chapter, we'll take a closer look at these channels and how they interplay with the way a person remembers experiences—that is, by sequence, time, or event. To describe how you sort information in real-time, I'm going to use a different set of criteria, but you'll later see how they come together to define you as a sequence-, time-, or event-driven person.

Sorting Styles

In *Rangers Lead the Way* (Adams Media, 2003), former U.S. Army Ranger and leadership consultant Dean Hohl gives a straightforward list of sorting styles (pp. 170–171). These are either-or choices. As you go through them, pick the ones that describe you and think of someone you know— someone you have a hard time communicating with—and pick the ones that you think best describe him or her:

A. **Large chunk** – big picture
    Small chunk – detail-oriented

B. **Sequential** – orderly, process-oriented
    Random – juggler, productive in spite of a messy desk

C. **Positive** – optimist
    Negative – pessimist

D. **Sameness** – picks up similarities and patterns
    Difference – picks up contrasts

E. **Past** – oriented toward what happened before
    Present – oriented toward today
    Future – oriented toward tomorrow

F. **I** – definite sense of self-worth and own ideas
    We – prefers confirmation from others

G. **Polarity responder** – offers alternatives, "devil's advocate"
    Conformity responder – more likely to agree than offer alternatives

H.   **Approach** – actively curious, moves
toward the unknown

Avoidance – inhibited, moves away
from the unknown

Let's say our suspected liar is kinesthetic, who is a large-chunk, random sort of guy and he's trying to impress you by talking about cars he's owned—or says he owned. His Porsche cornered beautifully at 75 miles per hour, it went from zero to 60 in a few seconds, and on and on. You, on the other hand, are a visual person, who tends to be a sequential, small chunker. You ask him what color the car was and to describe the interior and how much trunk space he had—and he fumbles. The lack of rapport didn't necessarily make you doubt his story but, when you pursued more information based on your access sense and your sorting style, his Porsche didn't sound so real anymore.

As an interrogator, these differences may help you spot a lie, but to extract information you'll probably want to build rapport with your source. Your baselining questions need to give you information about his access sense and sorting style, so that you talk to him on his own terms.

As these two tools of analysis suggest, communication isn't just verbal. Words are just one common system of auditory symbols to transmit an idea from one person to another. A handshake is a kinesthetic symbol. A wink is a visual symbol. Perfume is an olfactory communication. None has an absolute meaning. They can be misconstrued not only because of differences in access and sorting style, but also because people have connotations or idiosyncratic associations for symbols. These may have more weight in their mind than the denotations. For example, I associate perfume with flirting, probably because women in the military didn't wear perfume unless they were off-duty socializing. The first time I realized the important of connotations was in the ninth grade when my English teacher, Shepherd Chuites, announced,

"It makes me angry as heck when someone offers a home for sale in the newspaper. You can't sell a home. You can sell a house." The point stuck with me the rest of my life.

People can mean different things by different symbols, because each of us has *filters*. Filters are sensory, cultural, religious, ethnic, physical, racial—the litany can go on and on. A person smelling of cigarettes might strike you as careless, repulsive, and nervous because those are traits you associate with smoking. Subliminally, you might value what that person says less than the statements of someone who has no odor. That individual could have the most profound insights of anyone you have ever met, but your filters prevent you from absorbing his wisdom. Many people in the South, people who were my neighbors when I was a small child, could not see Martin Luther King for the man of greatness that he was. To them, he was black, so he couldn't possibly say anything relevant or inspiring to white people.

Whenever we do something or learn something new, it affects our filters. Whenever we make a decision, it limits another choice. Whenever we assign a meaning to a word, it defines for us how it can be used. In Arabic, the word, approximately spelled "qama," means four pages of stuff. It's too broad to move into this language—possibly approaching indefinable—so it serves as an example of a filter that will always come between people who understand Arabic and people who don't.

To illustrate the idea of filters to classes of interrogators, I've used overhead transparencies to reveal one layer of a picture at a time. By the time I removed all of the layers, the picture had changed multiple times.

You have to recognize filters and work with them and through them in applying interrogation skills. If someone is angry, she'll have a different filter in hearing a piece of information from someone who's fearful. A Kurd telling the same story about Saddam Hussein that a Suni political leader is telling will have a different take on it. Two lovers from your past, one of whom dumped you and one of whom you dumped, will probably describe you in conflicting terms. To the human mind, perception is reality, and so all of these people at odds with the information are telling what they see as the truth. "Truth," then, is not necessary what's true. You want to learn these techniques because you want to know what's true.

Choice of a word or phrase can enable a person to lie more comfortably, because that word or phrase distances him from an event. The killer's filters stop him from saying "murder"; instead, he says "accident." On a less dramatic level, your son might say, "Someone broke the window," which doesn't pin the blame on anyone—even though he did it—but it announces the event in a nonjudgmental way. Often, this kind of distancing involves putting a lot of filler words into a sentence and omitting the words that get to the point. Listen to any politician's denial of wrongdoing to find a vivid illustration. A more common example might be a drawn-out exchange in which one person clearly hopes that delaying a response will take the questions from a steady flow to a slow drip to a stop:

"Did you eat the cookies?"

"What cookies?"

"The Girl Scout cookies in the pantry."

"Aren't they there any more?"

"The Thin Mints are still there, but the Do-Si-Dos are gone."

"Oh, the Thin Mints are still there?"

"Yeah, but the Do-Si-Dos—oh, forget it."

One other thing to note here is that sometimes people deliberately talk without having any meaning in their words, but that doesn't mean they're trying to deceive you. It gives them time to set up an important statement, to delay saying something when it's clear the time isn't right, or to reclaim a lost thought. Politicians do it with phrases such as, "The American people need to know that this issue is one of many that we are giving serious consideration to in Congress." You might have used the device in trying to back-peddle away from a marriage proposal. And many of use have made sentences that meant nothing more than "blah, blah, blah" when we couldn't remember what we meant to say. It's a version of "uh" that gives a person time to think. I frequently deal with people in business who can't deliver a quick retort. My advice to them: If you think it's important to get in the first word, open your mouth with a rehearsed response, a space filler. You don't have to have your thought completely formed when you start talking.

Personality Types

The last set of criteria I'll give you for analyzing a person's approach to communication is the Myers-Briggs model of personality. The value of this is that it may be very familiar to you because you took the typology test at school or work. I'll give you an overview of the four sets of either-or categories and then suggest how knowing someone's profile will help you understand their approach to lying and how you might spot a lie. Here's an important caveat: I've used Myers-Briggs profiles extensively, but I'm not an expert on the theory. That's why I've asked Deborah Singer Dobson, a vice president of human resources, author, and certified Myers-Briggs consultant since 1989, for her insights on what a Myers-Briggs profile tells you about how to spot a liar.

Knowing Myers-Briggs types helps you establish how people think more directly than how they lie. Your ability to assess types becomes invaluable in establishing rapport and running approaches, which I cover later. A grasp of Myers-Briggs also gives you an edge when you decide to use someone's style of sorting data against him in forcing him out of a practiced lie.

Myers-Briggs takes four pairs of criteria to determine a type. A thorough test is the only true way to determine your type. The paired criteria are: introverts vs. extroverts; sensing vs. intuiting; thinking vs. feeling; and judging vs. perceiving. When determining the letter that is used, each in the pair is exclusive of the other. There are also degrees of each, so the test helps you to understand how deeply ingrained you are in a category. Certain generalities will help you get the basic idea.

Extroverts vs. Introverts

Do you get your energy from people or recharge you batteries through privacy? Do you prefer to focus on the world outside or on your own inner world?

This characteristic is all about where people get their energy. Introverts get their energy from being in their own brains and inside themselves, and they must recharge alone with their own interests and hobbies. They absolutely need their own private space and tend to need more privacy overall. High-energy introverts will often be seen mumbling to themselves when alone. They rehearse what they're going to say before saying it. They would prefer to watch any new activity and have an opportunity to practice on their own before experiencing something new.

Extroverts get their energy from the rest of the world and from being with other people. Strong extroverts will not engage in "alone activities" for long periods of time and find being at home, even when sick, extremely confining. Extroverts are known for "thinking with their mouths" and are known for literally making sentences up as they roll off their tongue. They must experience things and will put themselves easily into new situations and environments and tend to take on more physical risks easily. Their body language is generally easier to read than that of an introvert, because their body orientation is more connected to the rest of the world.

Sensing vs. Intuiting

This is the category that describes how you gather data.

Sensing types take the world as it is, look for data, like to build and make things and use their hands, and are generally highly organized and systematic. Sensors are viewed by others as the methodical and realistic, the grounded type who make decisions based on facts. Intuiting types can view this person as unimaginative caught up in the mundane.

Intuiting types "read between the lines" always and are using their "sixth sense" to try to understand what is not easily seen or supported by data. They are always about creating something new or innovative and generally are more comfortable with breaking rules if it means developing something new. Sensing types can also be very creative but generally try to solve problems that exist already or are attached to current technology.

As an intuiting type, I find my most brilliant observations come when I am talking to someone. I may not notice details of the exchange because they just aren't as important as the ideas that surface, and that I then internalize. Thanks to the Army and negative re-inforcement I got over relying on intuition, I can see the details of the concrete when I really need to. Not surprisingly, the Army is a sensing organization and, as with sensing individuals, often see intuiting types as flighty.

One time, I had a coaching session with four salesmen, two of whom were sensing individuals and two of whom were intuiting. The simulation centered on a customer who wasn't particularly happy. I asked the first one, an intuitor, what does this customer want? He said, "He wants us to build on a relationship of the past. He doesn't like or trust us, but figures we're the best thing he has going right now." When I asked how he knew that, he replied, "I don't know." So I probed further. He finally answered, "It isn't what I heard. It's what I didn't hear when I asked questions that made me conclude that." I asked one of the sensing individuals the same question. "He wants the product on time, a particular service schedule, and a budget that doesn't exceed $100,000." Again, I asked the question, "How do you know that?" He seemed to think that was a dumb question: "It's what he said!" The two types make ideal partners, but the sensing individual often can't stand the insights of an intuitive type, whom he sees as working from voodoo magic. On the other hand, inuitors get fed up with the nitpicking sensors who have to have every piece of hard data to make a decision. Their view is, "I'm smart enough to connect the dots. I know what this means."

As Deborah Dobson succinctly puts it, "An intuitive type most likely developed the microwave and VCR, while a sensing type most likely developed the heat shields for the space shuttle and better shock absorbers for cars."

Thinking vs. Feeling

First of all, thinking types obviously feel and feeling types obviously think. This characteristic is all about how people make decisions, and thinkers value the facts. They make decisions with their heads, whereas feeling types make decisions based on morals, values, and norms, and generally how decisions will affect people and how they feel or live. Facts may play a part in their decisions, but not the pivotal role.

Both types can get to the same decision, just by different methods. For instance, a T and an F who are married might choose the same car, but their reasons are different. The T will do the research to determine that a particular car is the right price, good size, gets reasonable gas mileage, and has an acceptable appearance. Those things may also have to be true for the F, but the car also has to make the F feel good. It might be similar to the car the F's parents had, and therefore represent something comfortable. The F would also want to be sure the car came in a desirable color and maybe even that the company itself could withstand scrutiny as a good corporate citizen.

Judging vs. Perceiving

This characteristic is all about how people want to manage their lives. Judgers—and this should not be construed as a pejorative designation—live their lives under the conception that there is a right way for things to occur. "Right" in this case means "structured" or "ordered." Judgers like their environment to resemble their mind: clean, orderly, and uncluttered. Judgers think of work first, deadlines with consequences, and committing to a cause, goal, or calendar. With regard to organization skills, these are the filers.

Perceivers, on the other hand, are pilers. Offices and living spaces can be a mess without disrupting perceivers. Schedules and deadlines are suggestions. Perceivers live in a world of possibilities. Making one decision limits others, so perceiving types are always rethinking or redoing things. Ps are procrastinators—not because they're irresponsible, but because they feel they have to wait until the last possible minute in case a really good idea or new information becomes available to help with their decision. They get energy from many things in their life "staying open." The proverbial person who believes that the perfect mate is just around the corner is most likely a P.

In Myers-Briggs circles, the joke is that Js make lists and use them, and Ps make lists and lose them. Js like to know many weekends in advance what they're doing, whereas Ps want to wait until Saturday morning to determine what they'll do that day, and then again Sunday morning to determine what they'll do then.

My last Army supervisor, with whom I shared a birthday, was David Hastings, one of the most knowledgeable interrogators I met in my Army career. Dave was a CW5, the highest rank an interrogator in the U.S. Army can reach. He was the scheduler and coordinator for all of our training—a classic J. Dave created all of our transportation grids and support needs. He also handled program coordination. On the other hand, I was the content guy and our front man. In Dave's words, he was the chartsy graphsy guy and I as the artsy craftsy guy. Together, we worked magic in the interrogation training because of our complementary methods and were able to create programs that brought in all services and foreign armies as well. Dave had a very orderly cube about 12 × 12 with masses of books, charts, and tables all in a neat row. He also had a sign on the wall that read "work until you fall down and then pick weeds." My cube was next to Dave's and about 12 × 18. You could rarely see the floor in it. I stacked documents to about 3 feet high, and all surfaces had paper at any given time. Once after a particularly eye-opening (for the students) training session about psychology of capture, the students identified him as the Palpatine and me as Darth Vader—the methodical builder of an empire, and the wielder of the dark side of the Force who was full of tricks and surprises.

Temperament Types

We get closer to an understanding of how all this ties in with lying by looking at temperament and intelligence types based on Myers-Briggs sorting. David Keirsey and Marilyn Bates did the original codification in *Please Understand Me*, and then Kiersey expanded on it in his follow-up work, *Please Understand Me II* (Prometheus, 1984 and 1998, respectively). With the Kiersey/Bates categories and keywords as a basis, Deborah Dobson looks to the four types—rationals, idealists, guardians, and artisans—for clues about how different people lie. Her insights reflect her direct experience using Myers-Briggs to help companies solve personnel problems.

The Rationals

The rationals are NTs—that is, a type characterized by the combination of intuiting and thinking. Kiersey cites their "high strategic analysis ability." In military terms, they are the generals. Their keywords are competent, autonomous, and strong-willed.

NTs don't lie well. They have a clumsy, confessional approach to deceit, first fessing up a little bit, and then spilling the whole truth in response to pressure. Dobson knows how to spot them: "It's been my experience you can tell when they're lying because they have fidgety body language, they stumble, they stutter." Because competency and productivity reign supreme for an NT, if you catch one in a lie, it's very degrading to him.

NTs are not accustomed to thinking that they have to lie because they are natural leaders; they think mostly about people doing what they say or want or being able to convince them with their sheer intellect or charisma. If they have to lie to move their agenda forward it makes them feel uncomfortable and is not a part of their "leadership persona," or self-image.

The Idealists

These folks are NFs, or a combination of intuiting and feeling types. According to Kiersey, their keywords are authentic, benevolent, and empathic. This temperament type's mission and focus is on "becoming" and harmony.

And they make good liars. When they anticipate having to lie in a situation, they use their gifts as visual people to conjure up a mental picture of the deceit—that is, how it would have happened. They have an ability to picture themselves doing whatever it is the lie is about, and that reduces body symptoms of lying. NFs are all about creating solutions, helping people and organizations. They focus on process improvement; therefore, they are always picturing the next step—something new, something that hasn't happened yet. They'll lie because it will maintain harmony and good relations.

Less-mature NFs are conflict averse and will lie as a result. NFs are also the "experts" at understanding others and what makes them tick, and, as such, they know what to say or how to frame things to move others to do things.

Don't take this to mean that NFs actually like to lie or prefer it as a course of action. In fact, they tend to be keenly sensitive to the morality of a lie. They just have a few traits that make them better at it than other classes of people.

The Guardians

These SJs, or sensing-judging types, are concrete communicators who collect data through external channels. They would then use a proven methodology to get people together to solve problems. They want to maintain the *status quo* and they value hard work. Kiersey cites their keywords as respectable, good, and reliable.

As a rule, SJs won't lie. They may get legalistic in an attempt to lie, but it's more likely that they'll say, "I can't talk about it." They are rule-oriented, so they avoid occasions where they might need to lie. They are generally easy to read, almost projecting guilt.

The Artisans

The artisans are SPs—that is, sensing/perceiving types. This temperament type's mission and focus are on enjoyment and action. They are concrete communicators who collect information from external channels and see the possibilities through their perceiver eyes. According to Kiersey, their keywords are graceful, daring, and adaptable.

SPs get you in the ballpark of truth, and that's good enough for them. They have occupations related to enjoyment and experiencing; they are pilots, paramedics, professional skydivers, and actors. Their approach to lying is "if I tell a little truth, that's good enough," which translates to "if you ask me what happened on the 10-yard line and I tell you what happened on the 50-yard line, I told you the truth. You have to keep digging for specifics with a lying SP. Finally, they'll probably tell you the truth, but, in the meantime, they won't get uptight about it. For that reason, they may not leak stress as a clue that they are hiding something. They can actually turn the lie into a game or have some fun with it.

•••

The value of spotting access senses, sorting styles, and personality and temperament types will take shape as you begin looking at the specifics of how to spot a liar. They will help you to understand how someone else thinks and where he or she is coming from to eliminate yet another filter from your mind.

Chapter 3

Are Men, Women, and Children Different?

Yes, men, women, and children are different. And the long answer is that people can be sorted according to how they learn, how they remember, how they relate to other people, and what they are mentally adept at doing. Some of these differences relate to gender, some to age, and others might be attributed to a genetic predisposition.

Are you a visual, an auditory, or a kinesthetic learner? What drives your recollections: sequence, or relationships of one thing to the next; time, as in hours and minutes; or events, so that some experiences come through clearly and others don't even get the tiniest bit of memory? Do you have a man's brain or a woman's brain? Do you take in information through the five physical senses, or do you consciously rely on that sixth-sense of intuition? Are you driven by logic or feeling? Are you older or younger than 25? Perception, memory, and your ability to express why or how something occurred all take shape because of the factors just mentioned. They also affect your filters for information and establish where you have natural advantages and natural challenges as someone who can spot a liar.

Even if you can identify these differences under the hood, however, you'll have a hard time using that information unless you grasp the commonalities between people.

Full Body Scan

I'll work my from head to toe to highlight the physical traits human beings share so that you will have benchmarks for picking out the different ways people telegraph deception. Human beings naturally look for patterns, so, as you progress to the techniques for spotting a liar, you will find that this basic knowledge prepares you to build on talents you've used all your life.

The Brain

A quick tour through the brain provides the foundation for reading and accessing cues related to eye and head movements. The visual cortex is in the back of your head, and you use that to process anything you see—it's to store visual information as well as to envision something. The sounds you conjure up or actually hear will be stored in your auditory cortex (temporal lobe), which is also responsible for motion and sits over your ears. This could explain why we respond so quickly to auditory stimulus as

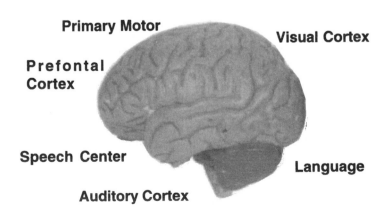

opposed to visual. It's a short trip from stimulus to perception. Anything related to higher thought involves the prefrontal cortex, or the front of your brain—what makes us fancy monkeys.

The Face

Unless the brain has sustained certain types of damage, the human face is the most easily controlled portion of the body. It also involuntarily leaks emotions in specific, easily identifiable patterns.

One reason why the human face presents us with such a range of possibilities for expressing both deception and genuine emotion is that it is the most complex system of muscles in the body, and an area where muscle connects to skin instead of bone. Watch Gollum in *The Lord of the Rings: The Return of the King* (New Line Cinema, 2003) to see how a face can telegraph a stunning array of emotions. The face of this animated creature illustrates his emotional transition from the pathetic, bitter Smeagol to the greedy, murderous character who wants the ring.

Shortly after birth, babies can recognize the characteristics of a human face, even though they see nothing more than gross shapes and shadows. In a study documented in the December 2004 issue of *Current Directions in Psychological Science*, when presented with two drawings—one, a circle with two dark spots below and one dark spot below, and the other, a circle with one dark spot above and two dark spots below—a baby fixates on the one that looks more similar to a human face. One conclusion you can make from this is that human beings are programmed from birth to read human faces. They are how we identify each other, how we determine basic qualities about each other. Even language reflects that with phrases such as "he lost face."

Face is our primary means of communication, whether or not we say a word.

The commonality of our facial expressions is, in fact, grounded in our animal nature and not where we grew up or what language we speak. Paul Ekman, an authority on facial expressions and their meaning, explains in *Telling Lies* (W. W. Norton, 1991):

> The involuntary facial expressions of emotion are the product of evolution. Many human expressions are the same as those seen on the faces of other primates. Some of the facial expressions of emotion—at least those indicating happiness, fear, anger, disgust, sadness, and distress, and perhaps other emotions— are universal, the same for all people regardless of age, sex, race, or culture. (p. 124)

A lot of body language, including eye movement, isn't nearly as consistent across cultures, races, and geography as faces. An Arabic proverb says, "To learn another language is to gain another soul"; this reflects the fact that language affects brain patterns. Albanians shake their heads when they mean "yes." In Asian societies, constant eye contact is not polite, but Arabs like to maintain steady eye contact. American culture generally associates eye contact with honesty and wandering eyes with some kind of deception, but that varies from person to person. We can find myriad other differences in body language, therefore, even among types of people who have a cultural commonality. Generally speaking, however, facial expressions are universal, meaning that human beings were designed to communicate with the face.

Given that we rely so much on our faces to convey intent, reactions, and so on, that means that we have more practice using our faces to communicate than we do using other parts of the body. It follows that we should be better at controlling our faces than any other part of our body in creating deception. We do have involuntary facial micro-gestures, however, that give away our secrets. You and I might be having a great conversation at a party. I'm smil-ing broadly at you and then I notice that a guy who beat up my sister just walked through the door. The remnants of a smile might still be there, but the corners of my mouth might turn down and my brow wrinkles. I was caught off guard and couldn't control my reaction; a noticeable in-congruence resulted. And even in situations where we have contrived and controlled the appearance of emotion on our face, our body naturally responds to stimuli before we have time to control it.

The Extremities

High stress impacts your body in the ways I enumer-ated in Chapter 1. The brain says, "Alert! Body, you'd better do something!" The body responds with, "Okay, this is my area! I'm going to protect us!" And then the cognitive part of the brain shuts down and lets the body take charge. Under emotional but less-stressful conditions, human bodies from the neck down still share a few re-sponse characteristics. The movements themselves aren't the same, but why and where they occur are.

Zoologist Desmond Morris posited that the hardest areas of your body to control are those farthest away from your brain—that is, hands and feet. People do lots of dif-ferent things with their hands to defend themselves, whether from physical threats or from verbal, psychological, or emotional ones. Whereas the arm and hand positions of a person in fight or flight are extreme and well defined, the hand positions of someone who feels annoyed, slightly threatened, enthusiastic, and so on differ greatly. What they have in common is what they mean.

You use your hands to accomplish the following, among other things:

- Set up a barrier between you and another person.
- Signal your superiority or inferiority.
- Drive home a point.
- Express openness.
- Excuse someone.

First and foremost, baselining is the most important thing in ascertaining the meaning of a gesture. If someone naturally crosses his arms, it means nothing. If the arm crossing only occurs when you ask a pointed question, it means something. One of the classic signs of self-protection, at least for a man, is to cover his crotch. No doubt, you've seen this posture of a man's hands folded in front of his body—the fig-leaf posture—perhaps standing in a way that makes him appear to be at attention. It's a type of barrier.

Humans are unlike most other animals in that we walk around upright with our most precious and vital parts exposed to the enemy. Every other creature on the planet, when prepared for combat, has its abdomen and genitalia safely tucked away. Barriers such as the fig-leaf posture, folded arms, and clasped hands are therefore invaluable indicators of discomfort. Other forms of barriers include a man who adjusts his shirtsleeves constantly under the guise of grooming. Unconsciously, he is taking attention away from himself and toward the activity while crossing his hands in front of the soft white underbelly. Most of the active forms of body crossing, such as nail grooming knuckle cracking and shirt adjusting, also include an element of displacement or relieving nervous energy.

One of the classic signs of driving home a point is *batoning*. In his public rebuttal of the accusation that he'd had an affair with Monica Lewinsky, President Clinton did this. He used his forearm and hand like a baton to emphasize every word of his denial. Adolph Hitler engaged in foot stamping and wild, animated hand gestures to whip his subordinates into a frenzy and his opponents into submission. Television evangelists commonly present outstretched arms and open palms to emphasize their point. A simple swat of the hand in the direction of anyone indicates they have been excused and are no longer of use to the conversation. Gestures such as these have become so much a part of communication style that vestiges of them will occur even when not intended.

Hands can signal a multitude of intentions and emotions, some exclusive to a culture. Among those that leak into our body language from the subconscious, the most prominent is steepling. You can regularly see examples on TV in interviews with politicians and experts. The steepler places the finger tips of his hands against each other and raises the fingertips to a vertical position. This is an indicator, at least subconsciously, that the steepler feels superior or has the upper hand. This behavior can be seen in all cultures and at all strata of society. A modified and bold version of this behavior is to place the interlaced fingers behind the head. Steepling in another forms indicates a feeling of vulnerability submission or inferiority. Place your hands in the steepling position and rotate from the fingertips up position to one in which the fingertips are horizontal or pointing down. In a February 2005 AP photograph, a welcoming Prime Minister Tony Blair greeted Secretary of State Condoleezza Rice with his hands in this lowered steepling position. The point may have been wasted on Secretary Rice, but not on me.

All extremities can unintentionally signal emotions; it takes practice to prevent that. Once in an interrogation training I was playing the role of an American captured by the enemy. The idea was to demonstrate to students how much body language leaked, and I had agreed to allow the use of physical force by the interrogator to simulate an unscrupulous captor. We had rules to prevent this getting out of hand; one was that the captor could slap me only three times. I played the role of a cocky jerk and when I responded arrogantly, the interrogator struck me. In the end my fellow interrogators critiqued my ability to hide body language. Their finding: I had raised the index finger on my right hand—as if to say, "That's all you get"—when the third slap came. I was completely unaware of it.

People use their fingers and toes to indicate significant things unconsciously. We routinely give directions and help make a point through the use of hand signals, so it is no surprise that we leak these when under stress. A person sequestered in a stressful meeting may point his toe to the door and fidget. Another may tap his wrist as the day winds on. All of these are ways the body uses its normal ritual to convey a message subconsciously.

The most interesting part of body signaling is that you can't stop it altogether. If you mask eyes and torso and trunk and hands it leaks in the feet. Even when you master these skills the real struggle is to keep cadence. Cadence and smoothness of transition will tell on you every time. A person who has successfully lied, and then realizes he has duped the questioner, feels a sudden rush of relief and may change his demeanor abruptly. Among the many ways it could show up are the speed of hand or foot movement, tone of voice, and cadence of words.

In summary, you can use your legs and feet to convey the following, among other things:

+ Set up a barrier between you and another person.
+ Express impatience or discomfort.

- ◆ Point toward the door, as a conscious or sub-conscious indication that you want to get out of the room.
- ◆ Signal tension.

Try to catch yourself in the act of rubbing your toes together, shaking your foot, tapping your toes, crossing your legs, or moving your leg up and down or side to side. What are you feeling at the moment? Would you rather be somewhere else, or with someone else?

Male and Female Gestures of Stress and Deception

For the most part, men and women don't have distinctly different gestures that will help you spot a lie, but here are three to consider.

- ◆ When a woman tilts her head, opens her eyes wide, and has soft lips, it makes her look vulnerable. Even if the woman is lying, she might be able to use this set of gestures effectively to arouse a man's protective nature. (Note: This has even worked on James Bond.)
- ◆ Women sometimes blotch in the neck in response to stress.
- ◆ When they're comfortable, men usually sit with their legs a little apart. If you see an American man snap his legs together, he's either feeling some kind of tension or he spent years of his life having teachers yell at him, "Put your legs together and sit up straight!"

See, Hear, or Feel Your
Way to New Ideas

Having looked at the body, I'm now going inside the head—where we start to see big differences in the way people absorb, sort, and store information. And all of these differences affect the way people both perpetrate deception and detect it.

"I see what you're saying."

"I hear you."

"I have a feeling about that."

These statements are the most common way to ascertain a person's access sense. Roughly 75 percent of people are visual, 20 percent are auditory, and 5 percent are kinesthetic. Teachers typically use a combination of visual and auditory in classrooms, but how many people do you know who seemed "stupid" in school and did well in the real world? I know of one woman who did so poorly in school, teachers deemed her learning-impaired—yet she excelled as an athlete and, later, as a personal trainer. She didn't have the kind of balance many people achieve. She learned kinesthetically, and most every other approach to education bored her or didn't get through.

For most of us, it's not quite so dramatic. But interrogators know that the difference in access senses still exists. It helps to determine how to make questioning more appealing, and it helps to know what can drive someone to the breaking point.

For example, an auditory person exposed to "white noise," such as the repetitive sound of children banging on a piano, would be in misery.

Your Memory Key: What, When, or Then What?

To extract information from someone through questions (as opposed to torture), you must know how he or she remembers things. Is the person time-driven, event-driven, or sequential in terms of memory?

Arguments will arise when an event-driven person in a relationship comes to loggerheads with his or her partner if that person is time-driven or sequence-driven. You get to church a few minutes late, but that drives him crazy because he must be on time. He gives you flowers at six p.m. on your first anniversary, but you were married at noon, so you wanted the event commemorated at noon. These differences affect our lives in countless ways. Take a look at complex recipes written by a sequence-driven person. You'll definitely know what to do next, but you won't know up front how long it takes to produce each segment of the dish or what the discrete activities are in preparing it.

With a time-driven person, I would ask, "What did you do yesterday?" and he might respond by telling me what time he woke up, when he went to work, and so on. An event-driven would tell me what memorable events occurred: "I met with my boss, had lunch with a client, closed a deal." A sequential person would provide a chronology of activities: woke up, had breakfast, went to work, and so forth.

The way you remember can be due to training as much or more than it is to "what comes naturally." Senior executives in companies often need to set their priorities in terms of events—product release, keynote speech—while other people around them concern themselves with time and sequence. Sports could reinforce or require a sequence-driven mentality, as in, "what play comes after that?" U.S. Rangers work on a clock. Their training stresses that an extraction

time of 0830 doesn't mean 0831. They will either have their
butts at the helicopter on time or get left behind. To emphasize this point, I asked Dean Hohl, author of *Rangers
Lead the Way* (Adams Media, 2003) and a former Army
Ranger, to tell me about his experience during the invasion of Panama in 1989:

> The night we jumped into the Rio Hato
> airfield, fifteen or sixteen C130s lined up, each
> one with 64 Rangers. The drop occurred at
> three minutes past midnight. Precisely thirty
> seconds prior to that, the Air Force dropped
> laser-guided bombs out of F117 Stealth Fight-
> ers. The Air Force had to cross the threshold
> going from ocean to land at an exact time in
> order to drop the bombs and get out of the
> area because we were right behind them. Once
> we hit land, we had a narrow window of time
> to assemble in our areas and press out from
> the center to the objective. Forty-five min-
> utes after the time we jumped, our re-supply
> aircraft were to land on the runway, a two-
> mile stretch that had to be cleared from ob-
> structions the Panamanians had put on it as a
> defense. The jumpers included a special team
> with hot-wire kits who had to get directly to
> the bulldozers and other heavy machinery on
> the runway and crank up the engines so they
> could move them and push other clutter off
> the runway.
>
> What if the fighters had not left their air
> base on schedule and had dropped their
> bombs fifteen seconds late? We would have
> had to parachute through debris or possibly
> have had to jump "danger close." What if our
> special teams couldn't clear the runway in

forty-five minutes? The planes with our jeeps and motorcycles, and other supplies we needed to secure the area and finish the mission could not have landed on schedule. That would have jeopardized the mission, and more importantly, jeopardized lives.

In this kind of situation, there's no calling the customer and apologizing. Lives depend on strict adherence to the timetable. We found out later that the brass had estimated that we'd lose eighty men that night. Instead, we stuck to the schedule and plan, completing the mission in a mere five hours and losing only two Rangers.

Depending on whether you are a sequence, a time, or an event person, certain types of lies are easier or harder for you to tell and defend. By the same token, certain types of questioning will elicit a calm lie of omission or commission, but other types will rattle the liar and cause him to leak emotion.

For example, let's say a sequence-driven person steals $50,000 out of the company safe. When questioned out of suspicion—"What did you do yesterday?—he says, "I closed the safe and went home." He simply picked up with the part of the sequence that was true, so the lie of omission comes out comfortably. If the question is, "What did you do with the money?" his response might be: "I put it in the safe and closed the door." That's harder for him to say because the statement doesn't track with the actual sequence of events. It is now a lie of commission because the true sequence is that he put some of the money in the safe and some of it in his briefcase, and then he closed the door. It takes more energy for him than the lie of omission, and he is more likely to signal that lie through his body language.

Event-driven people are big chunkers, if you want to use the information sorting nomenclature from the last chapter. They put things in order of what's important, so in responding to a question about what they did yesterday, they might not even mention what happened in order. Sequence-drive people are small-chunk sorters; one thing hinges on the next. Time-driven people have a sequence that dictated by chronology, so they are likely to remember how long it took for something to occur and what time the next event happened. It's another version of small-chunking.

Before trying to extract information, you need to ask baselining questions to determine what kind of person you're dealing with. After that, you can choose to undermine the person's pattern of communicating by using a conflicting style, but that could interrupt your progress. More often than not, you'll want to tap into the way your source communicates, not confuse him. For example, you might ask your sequence-driven spouse, who's on a business trip, "What did you do today?" What you really want to know is, "What significant things occurred?" but he hears your question in terms of a sequence of events that began when he woke up and ended at the point when you're asking the question. He starts with, "Well, I got up when the alarm went off, caught the morning news on NPR while I was shaving...." If you want to maintain a strong rapport so the questioning can continue, you need to just listen, even if you feel as though you're Archie Bunker in the sitcom *All in the Family*. It was a running joke that Edith would ramble in response to Archie's questions and he would interrupt her with, "Just get to the point (pronounced "pernt"), Edith." To be fair, I should note that the Ediths of the world go crazy when they're deprived of the details.

Pretend you're an Archie, as I am, and you're interrogating a person who remembers sequentially. You could redirect him by interrupting with a question about an event or time of an occurrence, but you run the risk of alienating him on a subliminal level, if not a conscious one. At that point, you might cause him to skew the data. You also might telegraph that you have more interest in one thing than all the others: "I wonder why she didn't care about that new bridge construction, but wanted all the details of my lunch meeting with Sherry?"

Memory is sketchy at best. You want him to remember items the way he logged them; the more you drag the person away from his normal thought process, the more liable he is to distort the data. Put up with a couple of extra minutes of blah, blah. It's easier, and more effective, for you to adapt your style of questioning than it is for that person to adapt his style of answering. That said, I will also give you tips on redirecting skillfully in later sections.

Male and Female Minds—Or, "Oh, What a Small Corpus Callosum You Have!"

Commonly, women remember things in terms of experience, whereas men remember what happened. Here's another generality that we use in interrogation: Relying on intuition, a woman can usually figure out that a man is on to her faster than a man can figure out that a woman is on to him. This is not to say that there are no intuitive men, but women seem to rely on it more naturally than most men. Look to the structure of the brain to explain this rather than Hollywood storytellers.

The corpus callosum is a thick collection of nerve fibers that connects the left and right hemispheres. Together, those structures make up the central nervous system's main component (the cerebrum). In general, men and woman are not equal when it comes to the corpus callosum: Women win the contest of size and development. Signals cross from the left to the right side of the brain (and vice versa) more quickly in the "female" corpus callosum. Men use the left side. Stop. They use the right. Stop. The effect is that men seem to persist in a logic pattern or a creative mode, whereas women might agilely flash back and forth from creative to logical to creative to logical, and on and on. Because intuition involves both feelings and facts, you can see how the "female" brain would support it.

Both men and women can be left-brained or right-brained, meaning that one or the other hemispheres appears to be dominant. Here's a scientifically questionable test to see what you are: Clap your hands together quickly and don't pull them apart. Which thumb is on top? If you're right thumb is on top, your left brain is probably in charge. If it feels strange to clap your hands and put the other thumb on top, then you are dominant one way or the other. If they feel equally comfortable, then it reflects an equality in your brain—at least in terms of which half is in charge.

Your eyes have different amounts of texture and color in them and can also give you an indication of which side of your brain is in charge. If your right eye seems to have more texture and flecks of color, for example, then you are probably left-brained. Look for texture more than color in conducting your observations.

Regardless of left-brain or right-brain dominance, men and women have different stress mannerisms—that is, they have different ways of touching parts of their body, as well as ways that parts of their body react involuntarily to stress. Under stress, a man tends to adapt by rubbing his skin (thighs, hands, and so forth), whereas a woman might flip her hair with fingers, tilt her head, or perhaps touch her neck. These are all auto-erotic gestures that redirect energy, but the woman's seem friendlier. In fact a woman's body language in the midst of deceit bears a remarkable similarity to seductive behavior. The key difference? When a woman uses these gestures to seduce, the lips are engorged with blood so they plump up, and in fact the whole face has a softer, fuller look. Under stress, the gestures might be the same, but blood leaves the lips so they look thin. Where does the blood go? To the muscles, because the person under stress has autonomic responses associated with the fight-or-flight mode. Men: Remember this signal when you meet a woman you find attractive and you'll have a good sense of what could, or won't, happen next.

We've seen a bizarre exception to this stress signal during interrogations. Some women find power so attractive that, even when threatened verbally in a fear up approach (see Chapter 6), they exhibit signs of seduction. Of course, a male interrogator will take advantage of that as much as possible to extract information (some feeling as though they're the star of a spy movie the whole time.) It's rarely true, however, that men find powerful women disarmingly attractive, so female interrogators take a different approach.

The key differences between men and women as interrogators show up during the approach and questioning phases of the process, which will receive much more attention later. In the approach phase, male interrogators can generally blend in elements of physical harshness more naturally than women, although the Abu Ghraib prison scandal showed that females charged with prisoners might use it, too. Depending on the circumstances, female interrogators might have an easier time building sexual incentives into their approach. The less-obvious differences come after the interrogator gets the source into an emotional state through the approach. The interrogator needs to keep the person in an emotional mode throughout questioning. This could require flashing back and forth between a logical questioning sequence and reinforcing the approach to sustain the person's emotion. In teaching both men and women, I found that men often get stuck in the logical, whereas female interrogators can learn to shift back and forth more easily, but tend to sustain emotion when they should have turned it off. The concept is that the two have to blend: Interrogators have to be logical with the questioning sequence while, at the same time, reinforcing their approach.

Exercise

Females generally have a greater ability to focus on details. If you believe in evolution, one way to explain the genetic origins of this is that it would be vital that a woman be able to discern tiny differences in berries so she wouldn't poison her family. If she did, she wouldn't pass on her genes. Men would be more attentive to big schema changes, to notice differences in an animal's behavior or a weather pattern that would indicate danger.

Ask three men and three women to describe the same event. Choose an event involving some emotion, such as a violent car wreck or a funeral. Just have them write a few details down without knowing which person wrote what. Read them and guess the gender of the author.

The Confusion of Youth

The brain evolves forward in the same sequence in which it shuts off. So children are not born with the ability to think logically; in fact, some studies have indicated that the brain isn't fully developed until about age 30.

Kids don't polish their conversation or their body language. They don't know how to deceive, and if you study kids you can usually learn a lot about their parents. They will do everything an adult will do with their eyes, for example, to telegraph a certain emotion. They pick it up by watching and listening. Why does a little girl who's confronted with bad behavior cross her legs, twist her hair with her finger, tilt her head, and say, "I don't know"? She's an itty bitty woman hiding something at that moment. How many times have you had a positive image of parents you didn't know well or had never met—teachers have this experience all the time—because you met a child with manners? On some level, you realize that some of that good kid is probably still alive in the adult.

In determining how and when young people are lying, there's a complicating factor: whether they're male or female. You can give a well-behaved, thoughtful child a healthy dose of hormones in adolescence and that child will overreact, talk back, and act stupid for a few years. Commonly in limbic mode, it's a biological struggle for an adolescent to make sense. The hormones ramp up the endocrine system with the result that this teenager is essentially in fight-or-flight mode.

A common problem in communicating with a teenager, or someone exhibiting the characteristics of a teenager—say, an adult in sustained limbic mode—is that he's likely to scramble information. You give strict orders to do one thing, but he hears another and acts on it.

As part of our efforts to arrange a cease-fire during Operation Desert Storm, we were making a tape to play loudly to the Iraqis holding down a building. We wanted to say, "Don't fire on us. If you do, it will be bad for you. We'll blow up the building." And then they told me to insert a phrase, "All criminals come out." I thought that was absurd, but we put it in the tape. Sure enough, about a hundred people came out of the building. In a highly emotional state, the mind tends to distort and generalize, and this is precisely what happened here. They heard "blow up the building" and "come out."

Of course, kids are capable of intentionally lying, but keep in mind both their chronological and emotional ages before you assume they're guilty of a deliberate act of deceit. As child psychologist Peter Spevak notes in *Empowering Underachievers* (New Horizon, 2000, p. 67), our internal defenses help us survive feelings that scare us, and kids who are stuck emotionally will commonly use a stock of defenses that result in lies of omission and commission. Specifically, he cites these:

- Avoidance: An attempt to get far away from an unpleasant event or situation to avoid both the outcome and the emotions associated with it.
- Denial: A refusal to accept something as reality. Because this is an unconscious act, Spevak draws a sharp distinction between denial and lying.
- Minimizing: A lowering of the affect or value of an act to make it seem less important. As you will soon find out, interrogators consider this a key offensive technique as well.
- Projection: In this defense, the person externalizes hopes or wishes, and that leads to a distortion of reality.
- Rationalizing: A distortion of reality to cover up mistakes or failures that will further erode self-esteem.
- Repression: "An unconscious exclusion from the conscious mind of objectionable acts, memories or ideas, so that the conscious mind is not aware that the offensive materials exists."

If we could only leave these defenses behind when we grow up!

Section II:

Tools

Chapter 4

Planning and Preparation

The Value of Planning and Preparation

Research and adapt: That's the beginning of your planning and preparation.

Planning and preparation put in motion a process that concludes with you getting the outcome you want. Taking a shortcut approach, such as only reading eyes or relying solely on body language, is lame. It's a shortcut to frustration and mistakes.

Planning and preparation mean securing background information on your source, knowing that person's rituals, defining your role and his or hers, and making sure the costumes and scenery create the right effect. Interrogation is theater for one. If you want to see how effective interrogation techniques can really be in your life, keep that in mind as you plan and prepare.

In the interrogator's world, planning and preparation constitute the major portion of the work. First, an interrogator creates a picture of the inside of a prisoner's head by linking bits of information about him. In teaching young interrogators how to combine fragments of information to get a picture of someone, I used the pocket litter exercise. I would bring a uniformed soldier forward and have him dump the contents of his pocket on the table. The wallet alone would contain enough information to build a profile. You know a lot about a guy with a library card, condom, pilot's license, blood donor card, and ATM statements. (Think about that the next time you put something away in your wallet.)

Second, the interrogator builds a plan of what she will do on contact. There is an old Army adage that goes, "Few plans survive first contact with the enemy." It's certainly true of interrogation, but I might also add that the enemy has less chance of surviving if you have a plan at first contact. That plan covers at least two essentials: what will likely motivate the prisoner to do what we want, and a questioning strategy.

An initial assessment of a source, whether that person is a prisoner or your boss, is going to be based on that person's dominant role at the moment. You can influence that through good planning and preparation, but this is precisely where many people fail in their quest for a particular outcome. In my vernacular, they invite the wrong person to the dance. "Boss" is not a characterization that describes an entire person. "Boss" is one role of many that make up that person. Thorough planning and preparation let you view the other roles that create the person, in effect allowing you to decide whom you want to dance with. Given my choice, I want to dance with the role who's no match for my skill set.

To illustrate how planning and preparation influence outcome, I'll give you an overview of the phases of interrogation that receive a closer look in later chapters. Interrogators have the results of screening reports to help indicate who the source is; your "screening report" is the results of your research. Think of this tool as X-rays that help a surgeon pinpoint what she has to remove—in this case, information.

Phases of Interrogation

To make each point clear, I'll continue the analogy of "interrogation as surgery":

- Establish control (or, put the patient on the gurney). In an interrogation, I might say, "Sit in that chair with your feet flat on the floor and your hands placed on your legs." In a meeting, you might begin with, "Please have a seat," and point to a chair on the side of table where you occupy a chair at the head.

- Establish rapport (or, administer anesthesia to drop the patient's resistance). The word *rapport* implies a positive connection, but in this context it could mean a negative one. In interrogation, rapport may refer a stern tone that you intend to maintain: "I know you have information about the suicide bombers and you *will* tell me." Depending on the background information you collected for a meeting, you may also want to establish a negative rapport: "Bob, your performance review obviously comes at a bad time." Normally, however, you'd go the opposite route: "Bob, you seem to be running in place lately. Let's talk about moving forward."

- The approach phase (or, cut 'em open). This is the psychological piece involving 12 primary tactics to make a person comply with you. You rely heavily on the background information you've collected, the rituals of the source you've observed, the role you've adopted in the interrogation, and the costumes and scenery that support your drama.

♦ The questioning phase (or, extract the pieces you want). This intertwines with the approach phase and begins sometime after getting the source into an emotional state. Throughout this phase, the source must stay in an emotional state, so you continue to use the tools that made the approach effective in getting him there.

♦ Follow up with questioning (or, stop the bleeding). If, during questioning, the source gives me what interrogators call *source leads*—he tells me something he's interested in talking about—I make a note of it and follow up either immediately or later, depending on how he reacts. You probably do this at parties. You begin a conversation with someone that moves down that path and then loops back to the original point.

♦ Termination (or, wake up the patient and tell him you'll check on his progress later). This is where I leave the source feeling as if what I have just done is not finished, but part of a process. I assure him that I'll be following up on the information he shared and that we'll be talking again.

Background Information

In military interrogations, there are three kinds of data requirements:

1. Priority intelligence requirements: "I need to know this now; something's going to hurt me if I don't find out what you know."

2. Information requirements: "I won't die if I don't have this fact, but my life will be a lot easier if I do."

3. Basic information requirements: "I might be able to use this to gain leverage over you, but there's no guarantee."

Know everything you possibly can about your target. If you plan to baseline and question a loved one, you already have a wealth of information. The challenge in that case becomes the fact that you have processed a great deal of data about the person through your own filters. You must adapt by remaining as objective as possible. If your target is a potential client or employee, you need to dig up anything you can about him before you walk into the room for the meeting. Then, in the course of the meeting, you use that knowledge to move that person or group toward the outcome you intend.

Most people don't use the free resources that are readily accessible to find out about people around them, including their friends. They walk into presentations with prospective clients completely focused on themselves: What am I going to say? How can I impress him? That will get you nowhere compared to the person who has collected in-depth background.

By doing a search on someone prior to a meeting, you can find out facts about the individual's personal life, as well as things about her business. It's relatively easy and cheap to find out where someone lives, for example, which will tell you something about her level of affluence, preferences, and so on. If your target has a small ranch 30 miles outside of town, you can safely assume she likes the country, animals, and open spaces. When you conduct a Web search on her, you might also find references to the Rotary Club or some other service organization; that will clue you in about her sense of community. All of that is important baselining information. I'm not saying that you should find out where someone lives and start talking about her neighborhood in the first meeting—that's potentially creepy. Find out what you can, make it clear that have you have good intelligence on the business, and then use the personal information you've collected to give you insights on the individual.

When I received an interrogation assignment in the Army, I read everything about that prisoner in the files. I examined everything that other soldiers had stripped off his body and put in a bag. Then, I walked out and watched the prisoner, maybe for 20 minutes, maybe for 10 hours, depending on who he was. I recorded everything he did— how he interacted with other people, what his mannerisms were, and so on—so that I would know later when he deviated from his normal pattern.

Let's say the prisoner was a chemical weapons expert. Because that's an area of strong interest, we would have had information on file about chemical weapons, even though we may have very few background facts on the prisoner himself. From that information, I could not only reinforce my ability to question him on his expertise, but also deduce certain things about him.

The impression I create with the prisoner by knowing about chemical weapons gives me credibility with him as well as an ability to question sharply. If I begin the interrogation genuinely ignorant of his field, I might say, "Tell me something about chemical weapons," and he could lead me down a path of irrelevant details and nonsense. He would know almost immediately that I had no clue about his expertise. If, however, I begin the interrogation the same way, but follow up with well-informed questions, he has no idea how much I know and I have the chance to lead *him* down a narrow path of fact after fact after fact.

In civilian life, this style of preparation has been invaluable to me. I walk into meetings with people I have never met and know the details of their business and maybe even their office operations—but they don't know nearly as much about me. This one-up position might stem from really simple facts. The person comes from Kansas, has a teenaged boy who just learned to drive, and loves baseball. Knowledge is power. I know more than they do and that gives me an advantage in a negotiation, interview, or presentation.

Now is where the information in Section I starts to influence your ability to spot a liar. Everything you know about a source will impact how you approach him. Using what you know about Myers-Briggs, say you've determined that your source is a sensing-judging type (SJ), driven by input from the outside world, using methodical processes to make decisions. To establish rapport with him, you need to need to create an environment that is secure and fits his needs. Remember that his keywords are reliable, good, and respectable. You will need to decide early whether he is secure or insecure and whether you will attack his conformity to his own standards or bolster his self image. That is, you need to decide to go with the type, or against the type. The approach you then select is the lever you will use to create certain feelings to get the source to talk. In addition to his temperament category, you also want to ascertain learning style: Is he time-, event-, or sequence-driven? This will become important from the minute you open your mouth to engage your source in conversation. The learning modality—visual, auditory, or kinesthetic—will also give you insights on how to structure your questions either to suit his style of memory or to counter it to cause stress.

Combine this internal background information on your source with the externals, such as education, residence, and so on, and you can pinpoint sensitivities and characteristics of a person to an astonishing degree. You will know with a great level of certainty how useful pride, emotion, and other elements of approaches will be. These facts also figure prominently into the scheme of data that includes baselining the person's body language and speech patterns. Taken together, they tell you what you need to know to build rapport and apply stress so you can drive toward your desired outcome.

The background information gives you an initial view of whom you want to invite to the dance. You refine that as you get to know your source. You know it will be easier to achieve your outcome in the meeting, for example, if you can draw out the relationship-oriented community servant than it will be if you draw out the cutthroat CEO.

Rituals

A ritual can be an automatic response pattern or it could be something you do quite thoughtfully. In some cases, rituals are habits "forced" upon you because of your culture or religion, or perhaps even a health need. Working fact: You adapt your environment to you through rituals.

Humans are designed for rituals. We use them to relieve stress, lure a mate, connect us to God, and make us socially acceptable. Sometimes, even when we can't quite identify a behavior pattern as a ritual, it often is. For example, I have a friend who grew up in the Roman Catholic tradition, which employs obvious and carefully structured rituals in worship. Whether it's a sacrament, such as Baptism, or Mass, Catholics rely on an identical sequence of events and words; this gives a lot of people a strong sense of connection to each other and to the Church. When she went with her boyfriend to an Evangelical Free Church without a structured liturgy, she felt really uncomfortable with it. She said, "They have no ritual!" I said, "Yes, they do. It just looks different." She insisted that wasn't the case until we looked at the service closely. Every week, they sang at least five songs. Every week, they listened to a sermon or some other presentation containing a Bible-based message. Every week, they took up a collection. Every week, they had a designated time for socializing. There were also lots of physical elements of the service—where the musicians stood, where the pastor preached, and so on—that ritualized the experience. Without enough of those elements, people in the congregation would get "lost." They wouldn't feel connected to each other, to the pastor, to the point of the whole thing.

Stress Relievers

The rituals of primary interest to interrogators are those that relieve stress. Watch how animals use ritual for this purpose. Some cats crawl under the bed when a stranger enters the room, and some circle the new person and smell her shoes. A parrot might pluck his feathers. "Behaving like a caged animal" has real meaning if you watch a captive creature, no matter what the species. Most horses at the racetrack will develop one of these rituals, or "vices" as they are known in that world. The vices range from weaving a sort of dance back and forth, to wind-sucking, in which the horse grips something with his teeth and sucks air into his stomach. The vices release endorphins, so they become addictive behavior for the horse. Human stress rituals do the same thing. In response to the unknown or high level of anxiety, a person will automatically try to adjust to her environment. The interrogator's job then is to note how the person behaves when under no stress and to get a clear indication when the rituals begin.

The historical underpinning of some of our contemporary rituals is fascinating. For example, I found it curious that I could be easily identified as an American when

I first had tours of duty abroad. Foreigners would watch me eat and know immediately where I'm from. Other cultures keep the knife and fork in hand throughout the meal. So why is it that most Americans pick up their knife with the right hand (even if they're left-handed) and put it back down after cutting something? In the days of the American Revolution, the separatists and loyalists argued bitterly. These people were neighbors who shopped, worshipped, and ate together. So they developed a ritual that averted stabbings at the table and we follow it to this day: They put down the knife after they cut their meat.

Personal history also lies at the heart of many of our rituals as adults. If you were a thumb-sucking, hair-stroking, or foot-tapping kid, you may not be doing that specific action to calm yourself in a tense business meeting, but you're probably doing a variation of it. The thumb-sucker might have a habit of bringing her thumb to her chin. The hair-stroker might put her hand on her neck. The foot-tapper might move his toes in his shoes.

Let's say you're a foot-tapper and I put you in the cloistered environment of an interrogation room—a place designed to ratchet up your stress level. Your comfort ritual will become a more dominant behavior than it usually is. In this artificially sterile environment, nothing is familiar to you at first except your weird little ritual. In a new business setting or on a first date, you'll notice the same adjustment. You will also see it when, for example, a neat person has to experience some social or business event in a cluttered environment.

As you try to reorder your position in the alien environment, you will likely observe a whole spectrum of rituals that help the person adapt mentally. For example, if I'm interrogating the excessively neat person who has now been subjected to clutter, he may start out by foot-tapping, but that habit might join a party of rituals such as brushing his clothes, buttoning and re-buttoning his shirt cuffs, and moving his fingers across the table to remove dust. He would try to order what he could, to gain control over the structure of his environment as much as possible.

I have a cousin who used to bite himself when he was a kid. Any bit of stress and his teeth would clamp down on a nearby body part. He clearly had to train himself out of that to avoid ridicule; he developed a substitute. As an adult his version of the same habit was reflexively bringing his hand toward his mouth. Only someone who knew him as a child would ever connect the two gestures.

Food, Sex, and Sleep

Food

Remember Pavlov's experiment with the dogs? Ring a bell just before feeding time, and the dogs' behavior becomes predictive of the meal. Dangle a treat in front of your own dog, and then take more than the usual time to give it to him. If you wait too long, the dog will salivate enough to drool. This is a simple example of a feeding ritual. We are not far removed from our canine friends in this sense. The mere thought of food can raise digestive enzymes in the stomach and increase salivation in humans. In filming a British TV special, our team of interrogators teased the volunteer prisoners by saying, "They are preparing your food. Can you smell it?" In fact, the volunteers were being fed standard Army rations, a high-energy, pre-cooked meal packaged in such thick plastic that the smell of food could not escape. That didn't stop the prisoners from imagining it. The intent of the question was to raise expectations. A subsequent delay in the delivery of the food created a displaced expectation, which made them more vulnerable.

By most anyone's standards, Army rations are disgusting, but, in the field, they represent health and home. In that way, even this kind of food is part of a stabilizing ritual. People who eat to excess tend to view food as the centerpiece of stabilizing ritual in their lives. Interrogators exploit the fact that people use food to stabilize and offer comfort items—tastier treats than the standard rations that everyone receives—as incentives for the prisoner to talk to us.

In some cases, you can similarly exploit a person's ritualized link to food. Establish the routine of the source you are talking to. If the person has heavy food rituals, use that to enhance rapport or to exploit his telegraphed needs. You can create a great deal of discomfort for some people by working through lunch.

Sex

I just compared us to dogs, so I'll move on to another species in talking about the rituals of sex: birds. Bird rituals commonly involve a demonstration ritual, followed by acknowledgment, and then a mirroring ritual. In humans, these dances become more polished with age, but the basics are there early in life. Two of the more noticeable rituals are proximity and mirroring. Americans reserve space of less than 18 inches for intimate contact. This varies culturally. If someone moves in past this space he or she had better be invited or it is a seen as a sign of hostility. Even in culture where casual contact is closer, the rituals of sex are demonstrative. Americans traveling abroad are often taken aback by intimate contact in the streets and see it as a sexual ritual. The truth is that the elements of American sexual ritual don't involve intimate contact and this is obvious to the trained eye. Simply holding hands does not indicate intimacy. Mirroring involves making the body move as the other person's, and in its subtle form, it subconsciously puts the other person at ease. On the other hand, the seduction dance involves overt mirroring done at a slow pace. Watch sexually attracted adults still in the stage of courtship and notice the exaggerated movements that seem almost lethargic. If you increase the speed, you would find the dance bizarre. Voices lower, hands curl to make each person appear less threatening, heads tilt, eyes are open. As a result of hormones pumping, blood flows to mucosa and the systems needed for reproduction—eyes dilate to take in the picture better, lips fill, faces flush, and everything seems softer. As this progresses the mating couple begins to match cadence and the ritual is complete.

When I was stationed at Ft. Bragg, some of my fellow interrogators and I frequented a large country bar. Most nights, one of our group would walk back toward the rest of us and start mirroring the behavior of one of the others after his unsuccessful attempt to begin the "love dance." All of a sudden, the obvious rituals of mating take on a comic or disconcerting meaning. Out of context, they appear contrived, or even robotic.

If you are in an intimate relationship, there are rituals you conduct on a regular basis that lead to lowering defenses and opening up to your mate. This baseline is well established. If these rituals feel wooden and something is out of sequence, it is cause for concern. This does not indicate infidelity, but it does indicate a change in the way the other person's mind is engaged. Stress impacts sexuality in tremendous ways.

Sleep

Anyone who has suffered from insomnia realizes the power of ritual in putting the mind at rest and the body to sleep. How your pillow is angled, the temperature of the room, which side you sleep on—all of these factors can influence your ability to sleep.

The routine you conduct before you go to sleep can indicate whether or not you're at ease. Interrogators and guards keep their eyes and ears on all prisoners in the cage to learn about their state of mind as they try to sleep. (By the way, this is the kind of help guards in Abu Ghraib were supposed to provide to interrogators: simple observation, not acts of wanton cruelty.)

Business Rituals

Companies and other organizations that establish patterns for conducting meetings attempt to embed a ritual into the participants that not only connects them with each other, but makes it easier for the boss, manager, or supervisor to manipulate them. It sounds sinister—and it could be—but the point is to try to accomplish the corporate mission as efficiently as possible.

Bring people from different companies together for a trade association or coalition meeting and you're likely to see "ritual wars." To some extent, they will drag their corporate rituals with them into the new arena; before they know what happened, the rituals clash and cause disruptions. *Robert's Rules of Order* can be useful in establishing a kind of neutral set of behaviors in that setting, but they only go so far. If the guy from Company A keeps his laptop open and wirelessly alive because that's how people do it at his corporate meetings, but the guy from Company B has been trained to avoid that at all costs, the meeting has an undercurrent of tension. The simple solution is to create a new ritual specifically for that group: "Today, we'll going to go through presentations for an hour at a time. No laptops. After that, we'll take 10-minute breaks to check e-mail."

Roles

The 202nd MI Battalion stationed in Augusta, Georgia, is considered a "strategic asset" for collecting intelligence, and it's at the complete disposal of the theater commander. For a while, their motto was "Semper Gumbi" ("ever flexible," but don't call it classical Latin). This describes a basic requirement for an interrogator and surfaces most obviously in how he adopts different roles.

What will you project to the person you want a straight answer from? How do you want to be perceived? Are you playing mother? Tyrant? Seducer? Analyst? What is the other person's role? Act as a predator, move as a predator, and you will be perceived as a predator. Act as a rescuer, and your source will respond to you as someone who can take him away from the predator.

Well, at least that's how it is in an ideal situation. The more thorough you are with all aspects of planning and preparation, the more likely you are to adopt the role and approach that match the personality and background of your source.

A big part of interrogation is not just adopting a role that benefits you, but overcoming the role held by the prisoner. What if, as a young kid, I had been sent in to interrogate a general from a foreign army? The process would depend on my moving into a role of authority and undermining his ability to maintain his role as a general. I talked to a guy who interrogated Saddam Hussein. Imagine the role coaching, never mind the other aspects of planning and preparation that went into that confrontation.

In rehearsal, even before the costumes and scenery show up, an actor preparing for a role might anchor key traits of the character in his head through a piece of clothing, speaking, or ritual he designs for the character. The villain twirls his moustache when he yells at the ingénue, who bites her lower lip in fear. Before a job interview, you prepare for the role of public relations executive by putting on a suit, straightening your posture, and smiling.

You have certain scripted roles in your daily life. You're a little different with the various people you know: mother, best friend, employees, lover, kids, and so forth. Does that mean you have multiple personalities? No, because all of the roles are facets of your own personality. Within those roles, you're consistent. A sudden inconsistency that signals a role change would cause ripples in your world. Nevertheless, you sometimes have a reason to adopt a different role or expand on the one you have. You were in the rear cubicle yesterday and a manager today. Last year, you had the role of a partner in your law firm, this year you own a deli and entertain people while you make sandwiches.

Certain roles you adopt stay with you for life. I was a career soldier and I'll always be a soldier. People who see me in a corporate setting see that regardless of what my title is on the organizational chart. Your roles could be similarly colored by something in your background or a fact of your life (you were a body builder, you're a mom, you're gay).

Changing roles to suit your circumstances doesn't make you a fake; it doesn't imply lying. Adjusting your demeanor can be simply part of putting yourself in charge. Adopting the right role gives you a way of controlling events and the flow of conversation, and of driving toward the outcome you want. Your role affects perceptions of what you know, what you can do, and even who you know.

The role you choose can affect your very survival, or your survival in a job, too. If your boss suddenly yells at you, he brings out the victim in you, unless you have the capacity to bring to the fore another part of you. It takes practice because stress hormones will take you down an emotional path unless you have practiced remaining in cognitive thought under stress.

If I haven't trained a part of me to handle a traumatic situation, if I can't play the role of someone in control under stress, then I'm just a victim. Other roles, such as Greg the Businessman, Greg the Medieval Fighter, and Greg the Horse Lover, are still in my repertoire, but they aren't any good to me. If I can call on Greg the Hostage Survivor, however, then he can come to the fore saying, "This is what I do well."

When Oprah Winfrey appears in public, she brings the mogul, the abused child, the activist, the person who has both been overweight and overcome obesity, the African-American, the glamorous woman, the philanthropist, and many more roles. She makes cognitive choices about which ones she projects and when, based on circumstances, as well as the needs and interests of the people she's talking with. She doesn't allow her guests, for example, to draw forth the roles she doesn't deem appropriate for the occasion. She does have a keen ability to do that to other people, however (although, I'll add, I've never seen her do it disrespectfully).

Even within the same role, you can have dramatic variations through changes in speech and body. It's logical that you make the changes depending on the circumstances. A cop in the doughnut shop doesn't sound the same as a cop busting a thief. Volume, cadence, and other elements of speech convey relaxation, commands, anger, stress, and so on. The non-language aspects of vocal expression, especially tone of voice, have a critical role in conveying meaning and cementing your role in the mind of whoever hears you. Moms and dog trainers probably know this better than anyone. Mom can say sweetly, "Please go outside and play," and you know she just wants you to have some fun. Or, she can make the same sentence sound as though it's a tenpenny nail stabbing your thumb. They're the same words, but it really means, "Get out of my hair!" The rate of speech can carry a great deal of meaning, too. Excellent teachers and motivational speakers do this to drive home a point. Their speech is energetic and fast-paced until it comes time to deliver the Important Fact. They slow down so...you...get...every...word.

Costumes and Scenery

Costumes

In presenting yourself as an authority figure to your sales team, you might wear a suit, but the motivational speaker who climbed Everest might command far more attention from the same people by wearing hiking pants. Your costume has to match your role to have maximum effect.

Again, I'll begin with the value of Semper Gumbi. You may be a guy who projects precision with your clothes, taste with your Rolex, and neatness with your clean car. But what if wrinkled trousers distract you from a conversation, wearing a $20 sports watch causes hives, and you feel desperate for a car wash after riding through mud?

As an interrogator, I learned to destroy people who must have that level of predictability in their lives—people who rigidly maintain control over their environment. The less flexible you are about externals, the easier you are to move off center and, ultimately, to break. And if clothes, cars, and other elements of costumes and scenery define you, you're locked into a narrow role, so you fail as an interrogator as well. In the movie *Something Wild* (Orion, 1986), Jeff Daniels plays a stiff banker who meets an outrageous Melanie Griffith. Scene after scene provide vivid examples of how difficult it is for a rigid person to adapt to new situations.

That kind of person is an interrogator's dream target for two reasons: Any deviation from his routine that he initiates will show up right away, and any deviation I force upon him—such as spilling coffee on his pants—will drive him nuts. That kind of person could also be his own saboteur in trying to apply interrogation techniques for two reasons: He may have a tough time matching his role to the source, and anyone who is aware of his obsessions has a certain power over him.

I'm not telling you to change who you are. I just want to point out that you may have limits that will make it difficult for you to either fully use or fully resist the techniques I describe.

In choosing your costumes and scenery as part of your preparation and planning, you first need to be aware of preconceived notions of certain images. For example, if you walk into a cold room where a bright, white light stabs the darkness and see nothing but a small table and one straight-backed chair, you think "interrogation room." That's because you've seen it on television hundreds of times. If I know something about you, whether it's cultural or personal, that tells me how to make the environment more intimidating, then I should change the scenery accordingly. The idea is to make the prisoner feel vulnerable. When I worked at SERE, one of my colleagues often adopted the role of a cruel guard, a dark creature obsessed with cigarettes and coffee. He would pour his coffee on the floor, and then he put his cigarettes out in it. He made prisoners sit in that foul puddle while he questioned them.

Scenery

Planning and preparation include every aspect of the stage you are preparing for your audience of one. If you plan to come across as the mild, non-threatening type, your environment must support this; if you portray the savage, that role also needs support from the stage and props. When Team Delta filmed The History Channel special

We Can Make You Talk, one of the volunteers was a bright young man who lectured at London University. On our interrogation staff, we had a world-class questioner who was a retired U.S. Army interrogator with SERE with combat experience in Panama. We also had a younger interrogator named Marshall Perry, who shaves his head and has multiple piercings in his face and ears. To illicit fear from the young volunteer, Marshall washed beer around his mouth, punched the wall to bloody his knuckles, and visited the young man in his interrogation room. Marshall used his size and all the props at hand to portray a loose cannon. The retired interrogator, Dora Vazquez–Hellner, moved in and won a confession by coming to the volunteer prisoner's rescue and gaining his trust and confidence. He later told us he thought she was the only intelligent person in the group and he feared we would really injure him, despite the fact that this was a simulation. Interrogators in daily operations have to improvise because they are often not in the most suitable environment for their purposes. When you go into a prospect's office, you face a similar challenge. You are not likely to have the capability to modify his environment—or can you? Is it possible to remove him from the safe zone of his office, thereby creating a feeling of discomfort that you then resolve by offering services to make his life easier? In the interrogation world the only limit is the mind. We use change of scenery to create the illusion that we are not the bad guys. We walk the prisoner to somewhere he has never seen. We tell him we would get in trouble if our superior caught us, so walk quietly. We lead him between the two sets of barbed wire of the cage so that he feels that we are on his side. So how do you change the scenery in a strange office? Use your imagination!

Scenery can have either a calming and welcoming effect, or it can have an inhibiting effect, which is what all barriers do. Barriers remove your ability to read body language, but you can also use them to help make yourself unreadable. When you're stressed, the toe tapping, finger rubbing, and foot twitching that always occurred during a math test will show up once again. Putting a table between you and another person can hide stress reactions—precisely what you don't want if you're the one trying to baseline. The ideal configuration is one that hides your stress and reveals the other person's. Most offices are unintentionally arranged this way. The occupant sits behind a massive desk and the visitor gets a lone chair. If it's your office, take advantage of the setup. If it's the other person's, find a way to bring the person out from behind the barrier.

Exercise

Think of 10 people you see on a regular basis—some close to you and some acquaintances—and sort them out in terms of rigidity in their costumes and scenery. That could mean suits and car, make-up and bathroom, lingerie and bedroom, uniform and office, and so on.

Chapter 5

Baselining to Detect and Apply Stress

The Importance of Baselining

In 1929, when the Geneva Convention banned torture of POWs, military interrogators had to develop non-violent methods. Some focused on the intimidating power of words. Words: Could they be the most powerful tool you have to make them tell the truth? Yes. You can use words to go deep into someone's soul, to create a psychic pain it's impossible to defend against.

To do that, you can't rely solely on parlor tricks pulled out of a psychology book or from a blurb by experts in reading facial expressions. Using fragments of such material is what stokes arguments that begin, "I know you're lying because you looked to the left and blinked six times." Looking to the left does tell you something about a person's state of mind, but not necessarily that she's lying. Traits of human behavior such as this work into a scheme of unconscious giveaways involving the face, voice, hands, and more. Ranging from subtle to obvious, the signs can tell you whether or not someone is practicing deceit—but those signs differ from person to person.

So you need to begin with baselining—that is, the process of determining how an individual reacts in a stress-free situation. A baseline enables you to create for yourself a picture of the person's natural communication style when talking about non-stressful topics, such as the best restaurant in the area. It shows you how that person acts when he feels he has control of his environment. Once you know how to baseline, you can detect stress, or loss of control, in that person with certainty. From there, you can proceed to the next stages: using the baseline to determine which of your words or actions are causing stress, and then increasing those activities to apply stress. After that, it's a direct route to flagging deception and extracting information.

When you baseline, you take the role of dance coordinator. You are setting up a situation in which you can invite the person you want to the dance floor. You gain a high degree of control in your interaction.

To illustrate some of the dos and don'ts of baselining before we go through it step by step, I'll begin with a couple of scenarios, one involving a stranger and one involving a spouse. The scenarios both show how Samantha Smith, an avid student of human behavior, approaches a business meeting in the afternoon and trouble at home that night.

Scenario One: Baselining a Stranger

Samantha walked into a swanky corner office for a meeting with a potential client, the president of a mid-sized company. She wanted to determine the prospect's level of interest in hiring her public relations firm. Other key bits of information she sought were whether or not she had competition for the contract, the duration of the contract, and if he had the budget to afford her high-end fees.

Samantha surveyed the room to familiarize herself with her prospect's trappings. She looked for diplomas and awards—possible signs of wanting to impress people—and saw a framed reprint of an article about him. The room furnishings and reprint told her this was a guy who wanted to project success. She noticed his desk had no paper on it, not even a scrap. "This guy must get things done verbally," she thought. "He delegates, so the paperwork lands on somebody else's desk." This told her that he'd probably expect her to deal with others in the company if she got the contract. Photos behind him told her something about his connections and interests: his wife and the Tower of London. Because the photos faced out rather than toward him, she wondered what he wanted the pictures to project about himself. That he's married? That he likes travel?

Samantha set about to establish rapport and continue baselining through conversation: "The Tower of London must be special to you." Immediately, the prospect admitted that he'd toured it five times. "Five times" told Samantha that her prospect appreciated something solid and long-term, that he enjoyed history. Her inner voice cautioned: Stay away coming off as trendy! She asked, "My favorite part was, oh, what do they call that curved structure where they used to keep the Crown Jewels?" Samantha knew perfectly well the answer was Wakefield Tower. It was a *control question*—that is, something she knew the answer to. It allowed her to watch how her prospect accessed visual memory when he was under no stress, when he had no reason to tell her anything false. It let her hear the tone and pace of his voice when he was at ease. He put his visual cortex in gear and looked up and to the left a bit as he replied, "Wakefield Tower. That octagonal chamber upstairs is magnificent." Later on, when she asked him to describe the product the company intended to roll out, she saw him shift in his chair, quickly look to the upper left, and then look to the upper right, and then down right. She concluded that the product might still be in the design

phase of development. Based on how he'd responded before, his movement in this instance suggested he was first
pulling from memory, and then doing a visual construct.
The glance down right, the emotion corner, indicated he
might be feeling stress. Right after that, he brushed his
finger across the desk, almost as if he were dusting it, and
then picked up the brochure Samantha had placed there
and moved it to a credenza. He had taken an action to
restore his space to its normal state—a way of relieving
anxiety. Samantha kicked herself: These are his little stress
rituals! I should have known better than to put a piece of
paper on his clean desk. Everything he's doing now looks
as if he's pushing me away.

Samantha had to move fast to re-establish rapport. As
the conversation progressed and she learned more about
what made him comfortable and what caused tension,
Samantha felt confident that the prospect would hire someone soon. She also picked up that he didn't have a good
sense of who else might be qualified to help him. "I can
close this deal right now if I'm in the ballpark with the
fee," she reasoned.

Samantha asked him how many people worked for the
company and he shot back a response without batting an
eye. She then posed one that required a little calculation:
"In a turbulent industry such as yours, I was wondering
how much turnover you've had in the past three years?"
His eyes took a downward turn toward the left before he
looked straight at her and said, "About 10 percent of our
workforce is people we've hired in the past two or three
years." When she approached the subject of his budget
for the contract, his eyes seemed to hang in the lower right
corner as he talked. "He has no budget," she concluded.
At that point, she saw both an opportunity and a challenge: He didn't have a clear idea of what he would spend

on the contract, but, as long as he had money to spend, she could use his lack of certainty to her advantage.

Here's where Samantha realized she had fallen short in her preparation. Because one of her key issues was his budget, she should have researched the company's finances. How much revenue? What did it spend money on? What departments seemed under-funded? What were their growth projections? She had violated one of the basic rules of getting what you want from a source: Walk in knowing everything you can about him. She had run out of time and had to leave without a key piece of information—or closing the deal.

The scenario captures the elementary-school version of baselining. It is the basics, which I'll flesh out with more whys and hows. For example, tiny differences in eye movement can tell different stories. When a person looks left, and then right, and then center, one process is taking place. When the same person then looks right, and then left, and then center, another process is occurring. After you get more exposure to the complexities of facial movements, trappings, body signs, and more, I'll return to this scenario and explore more advanced steps that Samantha could take with her prospect.

Scenario Two: Baselining a Spouse

A bit frustrated with her afternoon meeting, Samantha drove home. As she picked up the mail that had been shoved through the slot in the door, she sorted it. "Hmm, wonder why Bill's ex-wife is sending him a card. It's not his birthday. No special time of year." She immediately became suspicious that he had lied to her about not sending money to his ex to help pay for her college tuition. She concluded that this was probably a thank-you note. As she heard Bill's footsteps outside, she decided not to pick a fight, but rather to ease a confession out of him. His first words—"How was your day, dear?"—elicited an emotional retelling of the highs and lows of her meeting with the prospect. After that, she wanted to jump right into the exercise of baselining Bill in order to work him into a corner, so she asked a question he would have no reason to lie about: "Did you get to your 8 o'clock meeting on time?"

Samantha didn't even hear his response because she knew she'd already blown it. She had violated the rules of the game. First, she needed to leave her emotional baggage behind. By giving in to her emotions, she applied stress to herself, and that diminished her ability to control the situation at hand. Second, she presumed that Bill had a confession to make. Did she want the truth, or a story that met her need to feel smart and one step ahead of him? Third, in terms of baselining, she asked a question that was worthless, because the response was "yes" or "no."

The frustration that had begun to trickle through her after the meeting grew into emotional white water. She finally just confronted Bill about the card, which he opened in front of her. It contained a photo of his son at Disneyland.

When we return to this scenario, Samantha's enhanced knowledge of the tools of baselining will enable her to handle the situation with expertise. She won't act like such a fool.

Baselining is simply using the tools of interrogation to understand how the source responds in normal conditions. Even if we want to be hard-nosed, we want to institute ground rules ("control" in the interrogation world), establish rapport, and begin questioning. In the interrogation world, control questions come from data files we have created about our enemies. In Cold War days, these were extensive databases about primarily Eastern Block nations. Today these fact files encompass information about supposed friends and suspected enemies. When we capture a single insurgent and exploit information, it becomes part of a database. Your control questions come from other sources. They may come from something simple such as, "Where is the restroom in this building?" Your control questions may also come from something more subtle, such as insights you learn from a prospect's receptionist. You are reading the baseline response to a question when the source has no stress.

Facial Signs

In a real way, eye movement signals you looking for answers inside your head. Distinct portions of the brain process data in different sensory channels. The visual cortex, which handles visual stimulus, is at the back of the brain. The structures in the brain responsible for processing sound are in the temporal lobes located directly over the ears. Cognitive thought and problem-solving are conducted in the frontal lobe in adults. By asking questions that target a particular sensory channel, you can drive your source to access that channel. When the source accesses a sensory channel, the eyes will follow that access. The questions need to isolate a specific sensory channel, rather than engage multiple channels, and the questions must be complex enough to cause thought. "What color is your car?" is too simple. "What colors are in the tapestry above your mother's bed?" is the right style. By asking questions that target specific sensory channels and specific parts of the brain—visual, auditory, cognitive—you can drive the source to look toward part of the brain. You can do this exercise with anyone, whether a stranger or an intimate companion. In fact, try it out on a few people. Watch what happens when you pose the following questions, or similar questions that more directly match the intelligence and experience of the subject:

- What does your kitchen look like?
- What is the fifth word of the "Star Spangled Banner"?
- What is the square root of 39?
- What do you think the surface of Venus looks like?
- What kind of sound does a giraffe make?
- What was it like losing a friend to cancer?

Did the person's eyes move dramatically, or just a bit? In many cultures, evasive or erratic eye movement is considered deceptive, so a person would work to avoid it. This exercise demonstrates that eye movement is natural, though. The eye movement you noticed is an indicator of which part of the person's brain was activated to answer your question. When someone recalls info from the memory side of the visual cortex, I refer to that as visual memory; I refer to created visual as visual construct. Was it memory left and construct right, or vice versa? You can use this knowledge of which part of the brain a person uses to create a baseline. And then, when you ask questions that should cause the person to draw from memory and he deviates, you have reason to be suspicious. You can tear the lie apart by zeroing on the pieces you know to be false.

Although exceptions do exist in terms of visual and auditory memory being left or right, most people respond in this way:

- In visualizing a place they know well and can describe easily, they will glance to their upper left. This is a result of accessing the visual cortex located in the back of the brain. (In Chapter 14, I'll teach you how to use a combination of memory and visual construct to skew a baseline. You'll learn, in effect, to resist being baselined!)

- In trying to recall the fifth word of the "Star Spangled Banner," people commonly let the song play mentally until they reach the fifth word. During that process, they look directly to their left—that is, over their left ear. The question keyed the sensory channel for auditory memory, and in most people it is over the left ear.

- The process of reaching into the brain to try to calculate the square root of an unusual number (as opposed to one such as 64, which involves a memorized response), will take your subjects' eyes to their lower left. This is one that has been standard for all people I have ever questioned. Inner voice or cognitive thought are always down to the source's left.

- Describing the surface of Venus requires imagination, unless you seriously study planets. Your subjects will have to make up something, and as they do, their eyes will wander to their upper right. Again, they are accessing the visual cortex, but this time in a creative fashion.

- What kind of sound does a giraffe make? None, but most people don't know that, so they will try to invent something. In that process, they'll look hard to their right, accessing their auditory processor on the creative side. If the source says she has never heard a giraffe, then ask her what she thinks a giraffe sounds like. This may elicit a complex response, causing the source to go to her auditory memory for sounds of similar animals, then going to auditory construct to compile, and back to the center to describe.

◆ Ever watch people at a funeral? Many of them will have drooping heads and eyes slightly turned to the lower right. This is a position that indicates deep emotion; I've never seen a deviation of this.

The only documented exception to this pattern that I know of is in the Basques. Keep this as a rule of thumb for everyone else: The patterns for the upper tiers of eye movement are locked together so that you never get auditory up left or visual memory straight right. The only differences from the norm are which side is memory and which is construct. Auditory is always lateral, and visual is always up. Of course, I haven't baselined everyone in the world, so keep an open mind about deviations.

As I said before, you cannot judge a person's honesty solely on these typical reactions. Paul Ekman, world-renowned for his writings and workshops on "understanding the face," identified a major error in detecting lies that he calls the Brokaw hazard. Named for NBC's Tom Brokaw, it refers to an incident when, during an interview, the news anchor interpreted certain eye movements as lying. He was wrong. The pattern happened to be normal for that individual.

Another facial sign, but one that varies from person to person, is the smile. My natural, genuine smile is a little crooked, a sort of half smile. But when I'm meeting someone for the first time or smiling for the television cameras, I will give a balanced smile. Take a look at people you know well and notice the difference between their relaxed smile and the one they use as part of establishing control. Notice your own smile styles: camera smile, amused smile, seductive smile, smile of recognition.

And then there is the element of the face that the French call the "grief muscle," that area between the brows just above the nose that's paralyzed by a Botox injection.

Smile at yourself in the mirror at the same time you use that grief muscle to draw your eyebrows together. You look stressed, don't you?

I'll come back to these signs and other types of facial signs in teaching you how to use them in baselining. First, let's go through a few other exercises.

Body Signs

You are looking for barriers and leaking emotion in observing body language. Baselining will know whether your subject's folded arms and foot tapping are normal, or whether they are serving as a barrier and revealing stress.

Have your subject sit comfortably in a chair. Ask questions that move from casual to somewhat personal to prying and watch how the person's body changes as the questions become invasive. You might progress this way:

- How many brothers and sisters do you have?
- What kind of fun things did you do as kids?
- Did you ever fight when you were kids?
- Did your parents treat you any differently from your siblings when you were growing up?
- What was the worst thing any of your siblings ever did to you?
- At some point, you must have done something hurtful to them, too—reading a diary, or stealing a baseball, or breaking something on purpose because you were mad. What did you do?
- Have you done anything such as that as an adult that really made you feel disgusted with yourself?

Another approach you can take probes information more than emotion, but as the subject runs out of information, emotion (and stress) kicks in.

Again, have your subject sit comfortably and progress similar to this:

- Where was your favorite place that you went for a vacation?
  * "Tortola in the British Virgin Islands."
- Why was it so special to you?
  * "I got certified in scuba diving there."
- What kind of a course did you have to take?
  * "We had to do practical training half day and go into a classroom every evening for five days. It was really involved."
- What are the most important things you have to remember when you dive?

The questions can move to a level of complexity that can tax the knowledge of anyone except a pro or someone with an enormous amount of experience. When your subject reaches the point of "I don't know" or "I don't remember" and you keep asking questions, she's likely to feel a bit inadequate and might make excuses for not knowing and try to change the subject. Did she make any sudden changes in body position during the conversation? How is her body different from when you started?

Auditory Signs

Language is a combination of spoken word, tone, and pitch. If you've ever had a polygraph, you know that the examiner asks you at least one question to which you must respond with a lie. This is an attempt to baseline you on your pitch, tone of voice, and choice of words when you are lying. These three key elements of speech, and how they correspond to shifts if your body posture, signal your relationship to the truth.

Trappings

In the last chapter, I referred to costumes and scenery as elements of your planning and preparation. Here, I'll use the term "trappings" to differentiate between what you set up and the customs and scenery that your target has selected.

Military uniforms are a complex billboard of information about the wearer. Uniforms advertise accomplishments, time in service, where you served in combat and for how long, and with which unit you served. It can even tell you if someone was injured in combat. In effect, the uniform is a resumé for the wearer and a trapping of the first order.

Trappings tell you what a person wants to project, what she likes, what excites her, what she's proud of, and what she may expect of you. Clothing, furniture, photos, the size of a room, a house, a neighborhood—if the subject has some control over the choice of it, then it reveals something about that person. After a while, people may not even notice their trappings and your interest may take them by surprise. Questions about the trappings allow you to build rapport and establish a baseline at the same time.

A friend of mine spent 12 years as a consultant to start-ups dominated by engineers and computer software developers. Depending on their age, they wore anything from jeans and sweatshirts to khakis and sweatshirts. Their clothes projected disdain for corporate mores; they concentrated on "the work." When attending meetings with them, the consultant usually wore suits, the traditional emblem of corporate power and success. The costume highlighted her value. It said, "I'm different from you. I connect to the people outside your world, the ones you need to make your business work."

One of her clients had trappings that posed unique challenges and opportunities. It was a so-called incubator company that put teams working on different projects into a single, warehouse-sized room. Old doors served as desktops. The floor was bare cement. No partitions separated one person or group from another. If you could develop a great idea, your reward for working there was enough venture capital to launch a business.

At some point, client meetings generally moved to the well-stocked kitchen at one end of the room. A kitchen is the equivalent of a primordial cooking fire, a gathering place for friends and family having open conversation. It's also a place where people might confront one another. Awareness of what trappings symbolize, as well as how they look on the surface, offers a tremendous advantage. A kitchen could be the perfect place to close a deal—or not. It could be the best area in the building to discuss a project budget, or the worst. You would need to walk into that area knowing, through your baselining, what topics makes your client anxious and what he feels good about discussing. A conversation in the kitchen could nudge him toward greater anxiety or turn his good feelings into real enthusiasm.

Once, I had a job interview in a barren conference room containing a rectangular table with straight-backed chairs that had no art on the walls. It was probably a convenience that the interviews took place there, but I knew I had to "own" the trappings if I wanted the job. The first interviewer came in. I sat at the end of the table with my chair turned toward the door, so he logically took a seat near me on the side of the table. And that's how it went: me at the head of the table being interviewed by people who sat on the side. Subconsciously, I controlled the conversation.

If this had been a client meeting, where would I have sat down? Probably, I'd leave the chair at the head of the table for the decision-maker and simply sit near her.

Trappings aren't necessarily owned or decorated by the person. For example, if a corporate vice president conducts your job interview in an expensive French restaurant, consider why he chose that place. On some level, it gives him a sense of control; it relieves stress. The fact that it causes stress for you may not have been a factor in his thinking.

Baselining helps you in two ways here. First, it takes you out of yourself and gives you a measure of control, too. It gives you a system for stepping back from your presumption that the VP took you to Chez Chic to find out if you know which fork to use. (An issue you can avoid if you simply let him start eating first.) Second, just as Samantha used the trappings of her prospect's office to learn about him and his business, you can use the restaurant.

Now consider that you are the one doing the interviewing and you are baselining the candidate. You take her to your favorite French restaurant because everyone knows you and caters to you. The menu is in French; you're fluent in it. In this scenario, it's possible that the restaurant has the trappings of intimation for the candidate. You know there's a high likelihood that you will create stress for her. That's what you want, and that's what you get.

Hold on to this concept of the trappings of intimidation. The story of Ann that follows in this chapter shows how professionals use it to apply stress and discover truths and personality.

Trappings have enormous significance in our lives, no matter what our cultural background or nationality. Sometimes, without them, a person loses all credibility and status. Take a four-star general out of his Pentagon office and put him in a sweat suit on the street. Would you believe him if he told you the United States was about to invade another country? Take the Pope out of his Pope clothes and away from his Pope attendants. If he gave you a blessing, you might laugh and say, "Thanks, old man." Conversely, trappings can give a person credibility and status when it isn't there. Put a bright smile and good suit on a handsome man such as Ted Bundy and watch him get away with murder—at least for a while.

Rituals

In the previous chapter, I explored the nature of and reasons behind certain rituals. In developing your baselining skills, keep in mind that rituals play a powerful role in our lives in everything from sleeping to arguing to seducing to closing a deal. In developing interrogation skills, you must learn to spot them so you can:

* Detect stress.
* Disrupt the ritual to create stress.
* Establish rapport by mirroring the ritual to reduce stress.

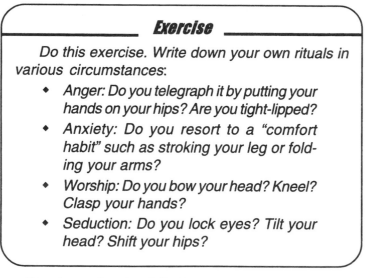

Exercise

Do this exercise. Write down your own rituals in various circumstances:

* Anger: Do you telegraph it by putting your hands on your hips? Are you tight-lipped?
* Anxiety: Do you resort to a "comfort habit" such as stroking your leg or folding your arms?
* Worship: Do you bow your head? Kneel? Clasp your hands?
* Seduction: Do you lock eyes? Tilt your head? Shift your hips?

(Exercise continued on following page.)

> *Pay attention to what you do when you go into a new environment, as well as what other people do.*
>
> *What actions do you take to make yourself more comfortable there? When someone comes to your house for dinner for the first time, what does he do?*
>
> *If you have children or are around them, you will learn a lot about detecting comfort habits by watching them. Children aren't subtle, and, once you become adept at watching adults deal with stress through rituals, you'll realize they aren't so subtle, either.*

The Look and Feel of Daily Stress

In Chapter 1, I listed some of the involuntary reactions you are likely to encounter or experience at some point, such as pupil flash and dilated facial pores. These are the extreme, involuntary reactions that you probably will never experience in applying interrogation techniques to your daily life.

At relatively low stress levels, you might notice emotional responses that involve deviations with the voice, eyes, face, and body posture.

You know from getting yelled at as a child that tone of voice can carry emotional impact. In addition to tone, other qualities can indicate stress, as in cases when a voice cracks or has a stridency to it. In baselining someone, pay attention to five other aspects of speech, as well: enunciation, word choice, response time to a question, elaboration, and trailing.

- ◆ Enunciation. Remember your mom or dad waiting for you in the kitchen when you got home after violating your curfew: "I want to make this perfectly clear to you...." Every word came out distinctly and, depending on how distinctly, you could gauge the level of stress. A loss of enunciation could be very telling, as well.

◆ Word choice. Someone who is uncomfortable may choose words that don't normally come out of her mouth. I have met people who select every word carefully. If this is practiced and not natural, stress will remove the capability to select words carefully. When someone changes the pattern from casual to carefully chosen words, it is likewise an indicator of stress.

◆ Response time to a question. You know those people whose conversation crackles because they always have an answer, and you know those people who seem to craft the perfect response before they utter anything. If you ask a question that provokes a change in pattern, it's fair to wonder what's going on. I have interviewed people who answer nearly every question by saying, "That's a very good question." That is a very good delay tactic. Rehearsed stories will have a very consistent response time. Identify deviation by interrupting the story to talk about something unrelated.

◆ Elaboration. Why would a person who normally blathers on and on with details suddenly give terse responses? Or why would a person who uses words sparingly become a chatterbox? The latter could be due to a few glasses of wine, but the change puts you on notice that something's different.

◆ Trailing. Some people trail their sentences normally, but others only do it if they don't want you to hear what they're saying.

Over the years of interrogating prisoners, I've also noticed that many people use end-of-thought garbage to complete their lies. It's as if they hit "insert" on their mental keyboard and added a phrase that had almost no link to the words before it.

Regarding cues related to eye movement, there are two big things to remember. First, people may vary according to whether they look right or left for visual and auditory memory or construct, but down left means calculation and down right means emotion. I have never observed a deviation in those. Second, the amount of eye movement does not signal deception unless it isn't normal for the person. I once played a game with my interrogation students called "To Tell the Truth," named after the TV game show. I had one person write a statement; he and three others each read the statement in front of video camera. I also taped the exchange of me asking questions and all four responding, and then showed the video to the rest of my students to see if they could determine the liars from the truth-teller. They all thought the person who had a lot of eye movement was the liar, even though he was the one telling the truth. His natural style seemed deceptive to them, which is why I chose him.

Pupils will also give you information on a person's state if they dilate or contract suddenly. The sympathetic and parasympathetic are at odds when this is happening. The sympathetic dilates and the parasympathetic relaxes, so flashing can be continuous or an immediate flash, and then gone. Excitement can cause dilation or pulsing, and so can stress. Your pupils dilate when you see something you like, too, and they will shrink to a pinpoint when you see something you don't like. Show a picture of a baby to men and, often, their eyes indicate indifference. Show the same picture to women and their pupils dilate. When we filmed *We Can Make You Talk*, I told a young woman I'd been interrogating that she was lying. I knew it because I had baselined her. She responded that she understood there was some voodoo theory about eye movement, but it was nothing more than theory. I trained her in eye movement through questioning and proved the theory to her. As she realized the theory worked, her pupils began flashing wildly.

Facial micro-gestures, some of which happen involuntarily, can be an excellent indicator of stress. I've worked for two people who had bad eye twitches when their stress levels would rise. That didn't mean they were deceiving anyone, of course, it just signaled to me that they felt a lot of pressure at the moment. Drooping mouth, arched eyebrow, narrowed eyes, wrinkled brow—all of these expressions can be a normal part of conversation for some people, whereas for others, they clearly indicate tension to some degree. And if you see someone start scratching his nose while you're asking tough questions, you may have just made him really uncomfortable. The human nose has an enormous number of blood vessels. Under stress, blood flow increases, and, as a lot of extra blood comes into the nose, it itches. Before that happens, you might see his ears get red. People blush in their ears before they blush in their face. If your ears get red, it's an indication of something causing extra blood flow, and that something could be stress.

Exercise

Think of five people you know well. Imagine their faces in a relaxed state. Do their mouths turn up or down at the corners, or is the mouth a straight line? Do they commonly use their eyebrows when they talk? Do they have any ticks or habits, such as licking their lips or closing an eye when they're thinking? You might find this exercise extremely difficult to do, even if it involves someone you see regularly.

Hands can help you adapt to a situation because you are uncomfortable. Picking at your fingers, curling your fingers to hide your nail biting—those gestures might annoy you, but they don't necessarily telegraph any deception. People who habitually use their hands in conversation, however, may be conveying deceit by gesturing away from themselves. Normally, the hands go up in front of the body, near the face, up and down, winding into a spiral staircase as they describe it, or palms up with a shrug when they want to express confusion. That same person telling a lie about where he found your diary might gesture to the side as he mutters, "It was out on that table."

Hands can leak a person's desire for you to go away or to stop doing whatever you're doing. Flicking a finger on a table or brushing the side of a hand on a desk could mean, "This meeting is over." You can even flip people off without using the middle finger or some other overt signal. Putting a hand in the air as if it's a stop sign may not be intentional, but it conveys a sense of "I'm through with you" or "Shut up."

With legs and feet, as with hands, watch a person to see what he does in a relaxed state. Detecting stress is all about detecting deviations from the norm.

Finally, how fast someone changes her posture either broadcasts an emotional shift or the fact that her chair is very uncomfortable. You shouldn't have a hard time figuring out which one it is.

Using Baselining to Apply Stress

Once you have baselined a source and know his eye pattern, body language, choice of words, comfort zone for contact, and other indicators, the next step is using this baseline to probe for areas of deviation that indicate stress.

Rule number 1: Don't let your own baggage get in the way. You may be a visual person, as

is most of the world, so you will readily notice facial and body deviations that indicate
stress. Don't forget the auditory and kinesthetic changes.

Rule number 2: Applying stress commonly
involves an interplay between emotion and
intellect. Maybe through physical discomfort
or an insulting remark, interrogators know
from baselining you that you will respond emotionally. Then they may move in with a question you have to think about, and the stress
triggered by the emotional experience dimin-
ishes your ability to think clearly. More stress
results. Or maybe they keep hammering you
with questions, requesting specific responses
that take you beyond your knowledge. As your
cognitive self digs for answers, your emotions
well up as you lose confidence. Again, from
baselining you, they know that if you feel in-
tellectually destabilized, you feel stress.

Sure, it's possible to put someone in a high-stress situation without consciously baselining him. In fact, people
do it all the time to each other by asking inappropriate
questions, yelling out of anger, and myriad other ways.
But in those instances, stress is a fruitless result of missteps and not exploitable. For example, personal space
differs from culture to culture. Americans tend to maintain a large space between ourselves and a stranger. With
people we know, we close the gap and stand squarely facing the person. When we really know someone, we allow
them to get within about 18 inches of us, with women tend-
ing to feel more comfortable than men about closing the
gap even more. When you invade someone's personal space,
you create stress whether you want to or not.

In contrast, when you apply stress for the purpose of extracting information, you must follow a deliberate path that begins with questions that enable you to baseline.

A friend recently related a story to me that spotlights how professionals in a non-military setting apply stress to a subject they've carefully baselined.

Ann did customer training for a computer company that developed custom products for government and large businesses. She earned a security clearance to work with the firm's customers in federal intelligence and defense agencies. Knowing that she would increase her income if she could apply her unique skills in an arena that required a higher clearance, she applied for work as a defense agency analyst.

In the two vetting interviews she went through, the interrogators used stress-inducing tactics that ranged from tiny to outrageous as they worked her into frenzy. Why would they ask a woman with a Ph.D., whose intelligence they had already complimented, if she understood concepts any fourth-grader could master? Why would they put a blood pressure cuff on her, and then cinch it so tightly that her arm turned purple? Why would they ask her where she had been in rehab for alcohol abuse when she told them honestly she never drank? Why did they strap her to a polygraph machine and then defer administering the test until later? Once, Ann concluded the session by yelling at the interrogator until she was hoarse. Once, she cried bitterly.

The whole time, she told the truth. Of course, the truth isn't what the interrogators looked for in this case. They already knew nearly every fact they needed to know about Ann. What they didn't know is what the vetting provided: How did she react under stress? Essentially, how long could she withstand stress until she imploded?

Among other things, the interrogators used trappings of intimation, including a small, closed room and polygraph straps, and a line of questioning we call pride-and-ego-up combined with pride-and-ego down. The latter technique is how interrogators got Ted Bundy to confess to more then 30 murders. Alternately stroking his ego and cutting him down, they provoked him into admitting that he had killed people they didn't even associate with him.

Were the interrogators just plain mean, as Ann believes? No. For one thing, they probably did not put the blood pressure cuff on too tight. When their questioning made her nervous, blood engorged her muscles and made it feel tighter. And when they asked her about drinking and she replied that she never did it, that signaled them that she might be hiding something. Using absolutes such as never and always is often a sign of masking something. "I never drink," might be translated, "I used to drink, but I don't do it now," or "I don't drink and I judge people who do very harshly."

As you develop your skills, remember that professional interrogators don't do anything by accident. I've adopted crazy accents and the demeanor of country bumpkin, and put mustard stains on my shirt to create an effect. Interrogators are actors. What they do is theatre for an audience of one.

Baselining Exercises

Objective: Detect stress in real situations.

Steps to achieve the objective:

1. Ask questions you know the answer to.
2. Observe responses.
3. Ask questions (you may or may not know the answer) that require speculation and may evoke emotion.
4. Observe responses; watch for deviations. A deviation signals stress. Be careful not to assume that fidgeting, for example, is an automatic sign of stress. It is only if the person

normally doesn't fidget, that is, the movement is a deviation from their stress-free habits.

Exercises in Applying Stress

Objective: Find out if a person is masking something. Steps to achieve the objective:

1. Baseline by asking questions you know the answer to.
2. Go into territory that makes the person uncomfortable.
3. Watch for deviations (facial, body, auditory, rituals).
4. Cause stress.
5. Probe deeper; pinpoint specific words, actions, and topics that increase stress.
6. Release the stress; go back to words, actions, and topics that are more pleasant for the subject.
7. Apply stress again.

In a military setting, the interrogator might repeat steps 4, 5, and 6 until the source has plunged into a limbic mode, breaks down, and then tells his secret. You might be able to do this successfully with a cheating spouse, too. In business, however, you have to be careful about the stress-release portion of the exercise. You don't want to take your subject into a limbic state. You want to recognize that emotion is welling up and go immediately to the release phase. It would be there that you make it clear that you understand what causes pain from him—lost revenue, bad publicity, design flaws in the product—and make it clear how you can relieve the pain. If you get someone to limbic in a business setting, you've destroyed the chance to build a relationship. You won't get the account, win the boss's favor, or establish a good foundation for team-building.

On occasion, you can tell almost immediately whether or not a person is masking something. If you ask a question that should require some thought and the reply is a snap answer, the quick response may or may not be a lie, but it is often a sign that the person has something to hide. For example, you ask a car salesman an off-beat question about the engine performance of the model you're test driving. Her quick, canned answer could indicate that engine performance is a real issue with this car, so you would want to start asking more questions on the topic. If you can tell that this line of questioning churns up some emotion, then you might want to switch models.

After you have established a baseline, you can tell when your actions, words, or questions begin to grate on the source or hit sensitive spots. In teaching interrogation I used the analogy—this is my NF personality style—of attacking a man in medieval armor with an ice pick. I can randomly attack and await the inevitable, or I can study his defense to determine his vulnerable spot, and then attack the areas I deem the weakest. Once I draw blood, I concentrate my efforts on that one spot. In your business life, you have to both find the pain and make yourself the cure, and in some cases that means making pain feel worse before you make it go away. This baselining and understanding stress are the keys to gaining cooperation in that business interaction.

In Army interrogation school, students learn what I would call a splatter approach: Throw some things against the wall and see what sticks. The throw is based on minimal information about a source and laws of probability. Using baselining gives you the capability to know with much greater certainty what approach to take and questions to ask. Interrogation school relies heavily on the students' capability to internalize the data and understand it intuitively. The technique I'm giving you is a process-driven approach that gives you far more predictable outcomes.

Chapter 6

Extracting Information

Time to go to the dance. Extracting information is the interrogation phase. The average person has consumed so much television and print representation of this process that he has a picture in mind of bright lights and dark rooms. That can work, but any room can be an "interrogation room."

All of your planning, deciding what information you want, how you will question, who you will be, and which rapport posture come together at this point. You are now a duck gliding on the water with your invisible legs paddling like hell. To breeze through the process:

- Baseline to detect how the source reacts normally and look for deviations that indicate stress areas.

- Evaluate the source for Myers-Briggs type and how he learns. You want to know whether he remembers via time, event, or sequence.

- Either calmly carry on your conversation or rant, depending on which role you've chosen.

- As you begin questioning, make adjustments according to memory and sorting styles. You may also have to alter your approach as you continue to learn more about your source.

Approaches

An approach is a concept of what will work on a specific kind of person in certain situations. It is a style of manipulation based on the target's desires, whether stated outright or suggested. The keywords that Kiersey designated for the four intellectual types will serve you well in shaping an approach. You want to take words such as "the guardian's"—good, reliable, respectable—and prey on that person's need for security.

Mental state plays a part as well. Assuming I know that a prisoner feels insecure and incompetent because of capture, I can play to that weakness, either by putting him deeper into his depression or convincing him that it wasn't his fault. My approach would involve telling him he had done the best he could. Whichever action I choose is intended to bring the role I want to the forefront. This is all determined by his behavior in the initial stage of the interrogation. Most approaches are not used alone but as an orchestration to better manipulate the feelings of the source.

In the planning stage, your approach strategy is based on personality—the background information you've collected, as well as your direct perceptions. The initial take on approach is based on external data. The refinement of approach(es) reflects baselining information collected after interaction with the source.

The U.S. Department of the Army lists 14 different interrogation approaches in Appendix H of its handbook "FM 34-52 Intelligence Interrogation." I take them down to a dozen because I think two are simply combinations of the others. The 12 are:

1. Direct.
2. Incentive.
3. Emotional.

4. Fear-up (harsh or mild).

5. Fear-down.

6. Pride and ego (up or down).

7. Futility.

8. We Know All.

9. Repetition.

10. Establish Identity.

11. Rapid Fire.

12. Silence.

I've cited scenes from a few James Bond movies, namely *Goldfinger* (United Artists, 1964), *Goldeneye* (MGM, 1995), *Tomorrow Never Dies* (MGM, 1997), and *Die Another Day* (MGM, 2002) to illustrate most of the approaches. James Bond serves as an inspiring example because he not only seeks the truth, but he also embodies the "Fleming flair," the kind of ingenious and offbeat tricks that distinguished his creator, writer and spy Ian Fleming.

A bit of foreshadowing: Approaches are not only the tool of the interrogator, but also a self-defense tool. I'll give you more on that in Chapter 14, but the movie examples illustrate how Bond uses approaches to his advantage whether he is the interrogator or the captive.

1.Direct.

You just ask questions. There is no emphasis on role-playing or driving the source into an emotional state. The Army considers this the most effective of all approaches (or at least it was when the handbook was issued in 1987), primarily because most prisoners subjected to it were enlisted personnel with no resistance training and no vital information.

From *Goldeneye*:

Natalya Fyodorovna Simonova: Who are you?

James Bond: I work for the British government. The more you tell me, the more I can help you.

Simonova: I don't know anything.

Bond: Let's start with what you do know.

Starting with her name and job, the computer programmer begins to talk.

2. Incentive.

Offer your source something he or she really, really wants, whether it's realistic or not. Food works well on highly stressed people because it is part of a stabilizing ritual. And then there are sleep and sex.

From *Goldfinger*:

We can only conclude that Bond used the incentive approach with Pussy Galore behind the scenes. In a convenient plot twist—after having some private time with Bond—she switched the gas disbursed by the planes from toxic to harmless and alerted Washington of the imminent attack on Fort Knox, thereby saving about 60,000 lives.

3. Emotional.

Using "love of (comrades, country, family, God, et al.)" or "hate of (again, fill in the blank)" can sap the logic out of a source very quickly. You use his strong emotions against him. Interrogators often use a hate approach when the source is a minority who may be oppressed and mistreated in his own country. This works well on some disaffected youth, too, if you can churn up their resentment toward older people having money and when they don't. Love primarily works with an incentive or a fear orchestration. The orchestration is to have contact, or protect the loved thing or person.

From *Tomorrow Never Dies*:

At a party, Bond chats with his old flame, Paris, who is now married to diabolical media mogul Elliot Carver.

Bond: Your husband may be in trouble.

Paris: If you think you're going after him, you're the one who's in trouble.

Bond: It's either him or someone in his organization.

Paris: And you figured you could charm the dirt out of me.

Bond: No, that wasn't my plan.

Paris: If it comes to a choice between you and Elliot, I've made my bed. You don't sleep in it anymore.

But after the party, at his hotel suite...

Paris: He's on to you.

Bond: Well we know where you stand. You made your bed.

Paris: I'm standing in your doorway.

Bond: Then turn around and go home. You can tell him you didn't get anything out of me.

Paris: That's it? Go home?

Her feelings hurt once again, Paris does the one thing (or one other thing) she knows will get Bond's attention: She gives him information.

Paris: He has a secret lab on the top floor even I'm not supposed to know about. It has an emergency hatch in the roof. It's the easiest way to get in.

4. Fear-Up.

This can take on two forms, either fear-up harsh or fear-up mild. What you generally see in TV shows and films is fear-up harsh: yelling, intimidation, flailing arms, in-your-face nasty—everything but beating. I primarily use fear-up harsh to raise the stress level and hide something else I am using. I equate it to pushing someone verbally backwards into a trap I am setting (the real approach). A fear-up harsh approach has no place in your daily life unless you want nothing more than a confession of guilt and you intend to end the relationship. My use of fear-up mild with a prisoner in the first Gulf War would have been a simple question: Would you rather talk to the Kuwaitis or to me (for example, the benevolent American soldier who will not torture you)? Sometimes, even a parent will do a fear-up mild approach: Would you rather discuss this with you father (in other words, the guy with the big fist), or do what I'm asking you to do?

From *Goldfinger* (fear-up harsh):

While Bond is strapped to what appears to be a steel gurney, Goldfinger explains that he will now show the power of his industrial laser that can cut through solid metal. Bond, in his calculated effort to establish rapport, thanks Goldfinger for the demonstration as the laser beam moves through the metal toward his crotch.

Goldfinger: Choose your next witticism carefully, Mr. Bond. It may be your last.

5. Fear-Down.

Your source is terrified, so you pat and console. You lower her fear though tactile contact and soothing. Once, I rear-ended a middle aged woman with my one-ton pickup truck and crushed the rear end of her sedan. She jumped out crying and screaming. I hugged her and apologized; she calmed down immediately. She was under high stress at home and her reaction to me was displacement of emotion, which made her a perfect candidate for fear down.

6. Pride and Ego.

This can take two forms, either pride-and-ego up or pride-and-ego down. In a pride-and-ego-up approach, you stroke the person's ego, saying things such as, "I can't believe someone as smart as you is only a private—your Army doesn't know what they have." This approach often works well on intelligent people. Pride-and-ego down can work on them as well, if you know their soft spots. For example, a colleague of mine tried to tear down a beautiful woman by mocking her figure. She knew she was beautiful so that didn't work. My pride-and-ego down approach had more bite because I knew she has less confidence in her brain than her body: I told her (as I leered at her) that I could see how she'd gotten into Oxford. Generally, the pride-and-ego down approach doesn't work with people who are lack smarts or looks, by the way. They already know what they don't have.

From *Goldfinger* (pride-and-ego up):

Bond: Fifteen million dollars in gold bullion weighs 10,500 tons. Sixty men would take twelve days to load it into 200 trucks. Now at the most, you're going to have two hours before the Army, Navy, Air Force, Marines move in and make you put it back.

Goldfinger: Who mentioned anything about moving it?

At this moment, Bond indicates through face and words that he understands the plan. He confronts Goldfinger about detonating a nuclear bomb to turn all the gold in Fort Knox radioactive for 58 years.

Bond: I apologize, Goldfinger. It's an inspired deal! They get what they want—economic chaos in the West— and the value of your gold increases many times.

Goldfinger: I conservatively estimate ten times.

Bond: Brilliant! But the atomic device, as you call it, is obviously already in this country.

Goldfinger: Obviously.

Bond: But bringing it undetected to Fort Know could be very risky. Very risky.

Goldfinger: On the contrary, Mr. Bond.

Bond soon knows what he needs to know.

From *Goldeneye* (price-and-ego up, and then down):

Bond: You break into the Bank of England and then transfer the money electronically. Just seconds before, you set off the Goldeneye, which erases any record of the transactions. Ingenious.

Alec Trevelyan: Thank you, James.

Bond: But it still boils down to petty theft. In the end, you're just a bank robber. Nothing more than a common thief.

Alec's ego didn't see this coming any more than he saw what was coming next.

7. Futility.

Star Trek devotees know the catchphrase "resistance is futile." It's what the Borg always said as they attempted to assimilate species into their collective. I told trainees that if they ever used that line, they had to look for a new job. The futility approach is used to convince the prisoner that resistance is futile, but not necessarily because of superior strength. The approach involves preying on a person's doubts, cultivating more doubts, and cashing in on your prisoner's growing belief that there isn't anything he could have done to prevent his capture or improve the situation.

From *Die Another Day*:

General Moon (to a Bond who had been tortured for fourteen months): Defiant to the last! Your people have abandoned you. Your very existence, denied. Why stay silent? It doesn't matter anymore. Things are out of my hands.... My son had an ally in the West. For the last time, who was it? Who made him betray his country and his name?

8. We Know All.

You go into the interrogation with as much background information as possible. Even if you know very little, you make it appear that you know everything. I also call this the "file and dossier" approach because I would commonly use a manila file as a prop. I'd hold it open and pretend to read from it and I'd question the prisoner. "We Know All" pairs well with "Futility."

From *Goldfinger*:

Here's an interesting reversal with the prisoner taking charge by tapping into the power of an approach. Keep in mind that Goldfinger's laser is creeping closer to a splayed Bond with every second.

Bond: Do you expect me to talk?

Goldfinger: No, Mister Bond, I expect you to die. There is nothing you can talk to me about that I don't already know.

Bond: You're forgetting one thing. If I fail to report, 008 replaces me.

Goldfinger: I trust he will be more successful.

Bond: He knows what I know.

Goldfinger: You know nothing, Mr. Bond.

Bond: Operation Grand Slam, for instance.

Goldfinger: Two words you may have overheard which could not possibly have any significance to you or anyone in your organization.

Bond: Can you afford to take the chance?

Suddenly, the laser stops progressing toward Bond.

Goldfinger: You are quite right, Mister Bond. You are worth more to me alive.

9. Repetition.

American interrogators rarely use this one. You just ask the same questions over and over in the hope that the source gets so tired of the monotony that he'll tell you what you want to know just to make it stop. Of course, it's dreary for the interrogator as well, so you want to take turns with a few colleagues or recruit a tape recorder for the duty. I've heard Brits use a well-orchestrated version of this one by getting the prisoner cold, miserable, and exhausted. The interrogator cranks up the heat in the room to shift the body's circadian rhythm—the prisoner's body automatically feels it's time to sleep—and starts out, "What's your name? What's your name? What's your name?" and on and on. When the prisoner starts to nod off, the interrogator will say, "Okay, Mister Smith, what's your number? What's your number? What's your number?" and, again, have the source keep answering until he starts to nod off. After that, he might ask, "What's your unit?" which is information the prisoner should not divulge, so he won't. But he keeps hearing the question over and over until he starts to nod off again. At this point, the interrogator says, "Thank you for telling me that your unit is the 43rd Infantry Division. Since you've told me that, let's move on to what your mission was." The source then thinks, "Did I tell him?" and may well start to talk because he presumes he's already spilled secret information.

10. Establish Your Identity.

If you have little or no background information, this can help pry it out of the source himself. You tell him he looks like someone else, a notorious criminal perhaps, who faces serious charges and doesn't even deserve treatment as a human being. In order to clear himself of that allegation, he'll probably say something that gives you a clue about his real identity and mission. I might open with, "I have a photo of you right here in front of me that looks enough like you that I could convict you of (name the crime) that happened last night." He might respond, "No, no! I was at a bar with my friends last night!" At that point, all I'd have to do is ask, "Which bar? Which friends?"

11. Rapid Fire.

You slam the source with constant questions that he has no time to answer. He gets frustrated with the process and finally tries to shout out an answer just to get you to listen to him. You trample on his answer with a criticism that he didn't make sense or didn't answer the question completely and continue the rapid-fire questioning until he can't stand it anymore. He tries to interrupt you by yelling out some information. I have found that this approach works well with more than one interrogator; the one whose question gets the useful answer then takes over and begins to speak in a reasonable pace. This approach preys on a human need to be heard and it requires a lot of the interrogators. You have to have a long list of questions in your head to carry this off.

From Goldeneye:

Defense Minister Dmititri Mishkin: Sit. I'm Defense Minister Mishkin…. By what means shall we execute you, Commander Bond?

Bond: What? No small talk? No chit chat? That's the trouble with the world today. No one takes the time to do a really sinister interrogation anymore. It's a lost art.

Defense Minister Mishkin: …Where's the Goldeneye?

Bond: I assumed you had it.

This comment provokes an escalating, rapid-fire exchange of questions and accusations, which Natalya Simonova interrupts:

Simonova: Stop it! Both of you! You're little boys with toys.

She then divulges the name of the true perpetrator and the fact that there is another Goldeneye.

Defense Minister Mishkin: Thank you. (Turning to Bond.) You were saying something about the lost art of interrogation, Mister Bond.

There's a strong element of "fear up" in this example, too, since armed Russian guards surround the interrogation.

12. Silence.

Silence is power. "Where were you this morning?" followed by dead silence will eventually elicit a response. Most people find silence extremely uncomfortable. The mouth starts leaking to break the tension, or the body may adjust in dramatic ways.

From Goldfinger:

Bond says absolutely nothing to the man guarding his tiny cell. He waves through the bars and then walks away. He comes back to the door and waves again, and then walks away. The third time, he winks at the guard and walks away. The guard looks confused, goes to the door with his gun drawn, doesn't see Bond, and opens the door. Bond jumps down from above the door and escapes.

The Army handbook names "File and Dossier" as a separate approach from "We Know All," but I see them as essentially the same. It also lists an approach called "Mutt and Jeff" or "friend and foe." This is one you probably know as "good cop/bad cop," and it's just an orchestration of two approaches to accomplish a pressure-release sequence. It might involve fear-up harsh and fear down, or a pride-and-ego down approach with pride-and-ego up. You can see this used for both dramatic and comic effect in lots of movies and TV shows with cop teams.

Questioning

You want to match the style of questioning to the source and circumstances. The types of questions could be sorted in this way: control, direct, repeat, leading, compound, and conjecture. In any given session, you'll probably use more than one type, whether you are relying on canned questions or a more interactive questioning approach in extracting information.

A *control question* is one you know the answer to. You definitely use control questions as part of your baselining process. You might also throw them into the extracting-information phase, though, to keep the conversation natural: "Really? How can that be?"

People ask control questions all the time to be polite, so this isn't a strange thing to do. For example, you know your friend's mother is extremely ill, yet you ask, "How's your mother?" When your friend's eyes go down right, then you can conclude that a down-right glance means deep emotion.

A *direct question* is a straightforward request for information that you don't have. In baselining, remember that you want to ask questions that elicit a narrative response, rather than "yes" or "no." In the process of extracting information, however, a direct question requiring a "yes" or "no" may be precisely what you should ask to get the information you want. Direct yes or no questions are very useful in controlling the conversation.

A *repeat question* is one you're not sure the source has answered truthfully, so you ask it again in different words. The more times you ask and in different forms, the more likely you are to detect deception and get the truth. Each time, it allows you to check the person's story and body language. Her use of precisely the same words to answer a question that's phrased differently can alert you that she's rehearsed that speech. A change in body language can tell you that she feels uncomfortable telling her lie again.

Leading questions are part of a classic questioning technique of journalists with an agenda. For example, "Do you think it's wrong that George Bush didn't show up for National Guard duty?" The direct way of doing this would be two questions: "Do you think George Bush didn't show up for National Guard duty?" And then, *if* the answer were "yes," the following question would address whether or not that was wrong. Leading questions have value in trying to control the conversation. You are trying to get past a logic point that you think your source will have an issue with, so you ask the leading question to change his perspective.

A *compound question* asks two or more questions at once: "Are you going to the store or the airport?" You can use it to trap your source, or at least catch him off-guard so that you generate emotion—that is, push him toward limbic mode: "Did you go to the party with her or put her in a cab and send her home?" We teach interrogators never to use this type of question because it creates confusion. When used intelligently and intentionally, however, it is a powerful tool.

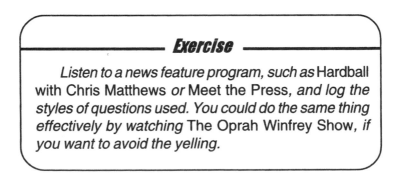

Exercise

Listen to a news feature program, such as Hardball *with Chris Matthews or* Meet the Press, *and log the styles of questions used. You could do the same thing effectively by watching* The Oprah Winfrey Show, *if you want to avoid the yelling.*

Canned questions, rather than being a style, are simply prepackaged questions of any style. They have the greatest value in matters that are complex or outside your area of knowledge. For that reason, canned questions seem more natural in a business setting than they do in a personal one.

As an interrogator, you ask questions that move down a path of complexity. You want to lead the source into an in-depth discussion that ultimately taxes his expertise to the limits. To do this, you need to do thorough research and ask questions that elicit a narrative response. Questions requiring a simple "yes" or "no" don't accomplish what you want.

Whether the person handles artillery, is part of an airborne division, or operates the radio, you have to be able to ask questions that stretch his knowledge to the limits—and then you keep going. You want to get to the point where you can say, "I can ask questions you can't answer and you're one of the best?" You keep doing this and your source will start to feel as though he's a failure, unless he's bluffing. And if he is bluffing, you can use your arsenal of detection tools to figure that out from the look on his face, his body language, and other indicators covered in Chapter 5.

You don't actually have to memorize a lot of facts to pull this off. If I'm interrogating a source about a nuclear submarine, I'm not going to know much about nuclear submarines after an hour of reading. But I can read enough so that I can ask some very intelligent questions about hull thickness, resonance of the metal, and more. Listen to interview programs with Cabinet members, scientists, and other experts. Journalists often rely on this tactic of developing canned questions to extract interesting details from the subject. Do you think most of them, who jump agilely from questions about biological weapons to a rise in interest rates, actually have a deep knowledge about all those topics?

In business, canned questions relate to profit margins, or hiring practices, or some other specific thing that requires you to remember details and to phrase a question exactly right. White House reporters come into press conferences with canned questions, and they sometimes use each other's canned questions as repeat questions. They will invariably do this if they feel the president has sidestepped a key question or given an answer that doesn't sound truthful.

In moving a conversation toward the outcome of uncovering the truth or trumping a business associate in a negotiation, good questions should be, first, clear and concise. The questions not only have to make sense to you, but to your source, so he can access the responses easily. Secondly, they need to elicit a narrative response. A question requiring "yes" or "no" only serves your purposes when you want to change the direction of the conversation, as in, "Do you know more than Einstein about this subject?" Use the seven basic interrogative—who, what, when, where, why, how, and huh—to stage your questions. "Huh?" is the polite version of "What the hell do you mean by that?"

Other tips for questioning include:

- Think before your open your mouth, no matter what style of questioning you are using at the moment. If you have a lot of questions you need to ask, but your brain hasn't prepared them properly, you will be as messy as a soup sandwich.
- Deliberately use a splatter pattern and ask questions that seem to go all over, but ultimately elicit the information you need. That's ideal if your concern is that you will not get straight answers from well-directed questioning.

- Ask the "next question." Don't ask, "Are you married?" Ask, "What's your wife's name?" Use your common sense on this one. If you see someone wearing beat-up cowboy boots in Georgia, it makes sense to ask, "How long have you been riding?" But you wouldn't try to jump-start a conversation with that question if your source is wearing shiny boots in a Manhattan boardroom.

Certain other types of questions serve the purpose of antagonizing and/or confusing. If that's the direction you want to go, then here's some guidance:

- No-win questions can quickly put your source into limbic mode: "Do you expect me to believe all this crap?" "How long do you expect me to wait for you to say nothing?"
- Leading questions imply judgment, and the more judgment they imply, the more annoying they become: "Is it true you've been living in sin for a year?"
- Compound questions make you sound either stupid or careless. If you want to come across as either or both as a way of disarming someone, then use them.
- Vague questions get you vague answers. They are useless if you're trying to get information, but helpful if you want to take someone down a parallel path to disguise your main point: "When you went to the hotel, did it seem like there were a lot of people just hanging out in the lobby?" Fuzzy questions and answers may serve you best as a self-defense mechanism. When someone asks a direct question, ask an open-ended, confusing question in response.

He thinks he's getting information, but it's only remotely related to the question: "How many people were in the lobby?" "Do you want me to count the people who work there, or the guests, or what?"

The Basic Mechanics of Breaking a Liar

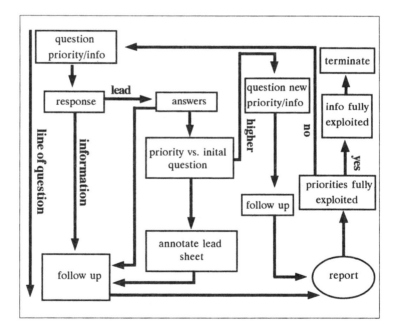

Questioning Chart: The response to the question provides either information or a lead. The lead meets a priority need, information requirement, or it dead ends. Follow the lead; determine whether or not it yields something of higher importance than the initial question. If lower, make a note and go back to follow-up on the original question. If higher, follow that line of questioning. At some point, you have followed-up on all leads and information; terminate the questioning. If you haven't fully exploited what the person knows, return to the beginning.

Refer again to Chapter 2 about the types of lies and the people who are most likely to succeed with them. Fundamentally, the breakdown is between people who store information with a lot of sequential or chronological detail and those who do not—big picture versus detail. The steps to using questioning to break a liar, then, could be summarized in this way:

- Ask questions that force the person into an uncomfortable relationship with the information he's just presented. A time-driven person who cannot account for half an hour is "caught." And even if you don't pick up the discrepancy right away, he knows it exists and it will affect his body language. This doesn't mean you confront the person with a conflicting style—you don't push the event-driven person into a time discussion, for instance—but rather you mimic his style and probe for greater and greater detail within that style.

- Involve someone else in the story. The liar says she was in her office all day, so you casually ask whether her assistant, who's been out on maternity leave, is back yet or her temporary replacement was there again today. People don't like to include other people in their lies because it opens opportunities for the story to fall apart. Even if it's a simple embellishment such as "I shot a 92 at the course today," a question such as, "Who'd you play with?" can make the liar uneasy. You might even see a blush in the ears or cheeks. By the way, animals don't blush out of embarrassment; the reaction is a distinctly human expression of moral consciousness.

♦ Tap into the person's access sense. Visual people won't remember conversations as well as auditory people. Auditory people will not have the keen recollections about what some-one wore or what paintings were on the wall. Kinesthetic people may remember the tem-perature of the air when they did something, but not what day it was. Again, establish rap-port by using the terms that relate to the liar's access sense; draw the story out in a way that's natural for her.

♦ Ask a *conjecture question* if, even after baselining, you have a strong gut reaction that the person is lying to you: "What do you think would happen if...?" When you ask that ques-tion, if he doesn't deviate from his baseline for memory, it means the person has studied the story and is prepared for a range of ques-tions related to it. He's covering.

Minimizing

Minimizing works in two ways:

1. You tell the person that, by comparison, what he did was not so bad. Instead of, "What hap-pened to the cookie jar?" when you see it in 38 pieces on the floor, you comment, "Gosh, I wish I hadn't put that cookie jar so close to the edge of the counter." You then assume a little bit of the blame, so that the "confession" about accidentally knocking the cookie jar comes tumbling out. The other issue, of course, is that all the cookies have disappeared and someone must be responsible for that, too. In the case of a crime, detectives might place a bit of blame on society: "It's terrible to see

someone suffer like that. People are driven
to help in whatever way they can. At least the
pillow over her face is a humane way to do it.
I interviewed someone last week who used a
hatchet."

2. You accuse the person of something far worse
than what you think he did, so that he admits
to a lesser offense. One way to use this device is to attack with the worse accusation
possible: "You're cheating on me! I know it—
I saw your car outside the motel!" "No! I've
been loaning my car to my brother on Thurs-
days so he can meet his mistress without his
wife catching him." The person readily admits to a comparatively small offense to avoid
the perception that he did something worse.
In a criminal case, it might involve the detec-
tive saying, "We have videotape of you at the
scene of the murder." The criminal then blurts
out: "I didn't kill her. I just watched."

Media coverage of the 2004 arrest of an intelligence
officer—a 15 year veteran of the Army Reserve—indicated
that minimizing probably played a key role. The accused
should have understood its value from his own interrogation experience; ironically, it may have been the technique
police used effectively to ensnare him. The self-described
human intelligence collector, who was called to active duty
after the September 11th terrorist attacks, allegedly sent
pornographic pictures to an FBI agent posing as a 15-year-
old boy. Upon getting caught, he declared he wasn't a homosexual, just curious about same-sex relationships. He
also said he didn't trade the pornographic photos while he
was on active duty, and that he used his home computer,
not military equipment.

I can imagine the style of interrogation that *may* have led to these assertions, and that is a series of questions and comments designed to play down the offense so he would admit his guilt. Something such as: "At least you didn't do this with the Army's equipment. That could mean life in prison because the military is very strict on that. Help me establish a time line to show you did this from home on your own time, with your own computer." And, "Nothing in your background tells me you're a homosexual. The Army doesn't think you're a homosexual. I'm just wondering why you sent those pictures?"

In interrogation situations, I've also used minimizing to provoke a specific action, not just to get a verbal admission of something. In a video for The History Channel titled *We Can Make You Talk*, my objective was to get a copy of a "prisoner's" signature. *We Can Make You Talk* simulated the experience of capture and interrogation with volunteers, who had information about covert activities related to a fictional operative. One of the things these volunteers had been told absolutely is "don't sign anything they give you." So after a few hours of exposure to white noise, variations in temperature, and stress positions— kneeling with hands in the air, leaning against a wall with the legs in a bent position—I eased into getting a signature this way:

"Are you willing to prove to me that you're really telling the truth? That you're not lying?

"Yes."

"I need to verify what you're saying. Are you willing to sign a statement that you write that just says you're telling the truth?" She wrote down the details of her cover story and said nothing about her mission.

"Put your initials on this. Right here." I told her. I was starting to train her. "And here." Every time she initialed anything, it was a sign she was becoming compliant. Soon, I got a copy of her signature as well as other samples of her handwriting. In this example, minimizing involved asking her to perform an action that was not in violation of what she'd been told—it was "less than." I didn't hand her a statement to sign; she wrote a few sentences and initialed them. That done, I had no problem getting her to write more and more.

Overcoming Logical Objection

When I create a chain of logic to convince the source that my answer is the right one, I take into account the way the person thinks—and feels. If I am arguing with someone who doesn't have a logical mind, I may have an easier time slipping logic past him. Anything that violates his feeling of right and wrong, however, is another issue, because he's probably a person who follows his heart. Myers-Briggs is useful here in determining the basics for how the person collects data and makes decisions as well as his general bent on life.

Assuming I have chain of logic that is flawless with the exception of one piece, I simply walk through the flawless pieces one at a time. Just before I get to the flawed step, I raise the person's anxiety to get him out of a logical mind. In the interrogation world, I do this through high limbic arousal, possibly by yelling. In business, this is not acceptable, so I would probe the pain of the person, bring that to the front, and tie the outcome of my flawed logic to easing his or her pain. This is the daily-life equivalent of taking a prisoner down to two choices: "mine and yours" or "bad," a technique called paring the options.

In the reactionary mode of high stress, people lead with their weakest Myers-Briggs style, not their strongest. You can therefore force a person into high stress, and then use the words of their true style (for example, good, reliable, respectable) against them. You remind them of how they think to box them into a corner. For example, my target is a sensor/judger personality type who is under high stress to get something completed by a deadline; his career is on the line. Because of his stress level, he relies on a flip side—intuiting—and starts calling on his gut feelings to make the deadline. I simply point out the facts and say, "To reach a reliable conclusion, we must take the facts into account and do the right thing." These words are his mantra, so he agrees. After I gloss over the ugly duckling, I take him through my next few logical steps and voilá: He agrees with something he normally would find objectionable.

Phases of Interrogation

The six phases of interrogation weave in your base lining skills, as well as what you explored in this chapter on approaches, questioning, and minimizing. When you begin the process of extracting information, all of your ghosts come with you: the red-haired boy with big ears, the child of poverty, the studious teenager, the flirt. These parts of you filter your images, your listening, the way you deal with you. You have to think past them in evaluating both the information and the person in front of you.

Establish Control

In real life, you don't get to make up all the rules of engagement about where your source sits and whether or not he's allowed to finish sentences. Nevertheless, you have ample opportunity to establish control by taking steps up front to influence environment and conversation.

First, handle all the elements of planning and preparation: rituals, roles, background information, costumes, scenery. Regarding the latter, make sure you know where the meeting will be. When important information is at stake don't choose a spot randomly, as in, "Let's meet for coffee some-where on 42nd Street." Your potential to take control drops if you don't know anything about seating arrangements and ambiance.

Your second step is to come into the interaction with-out emotion. Whether in business or love, you don't want the emotional party in charge.

A friend of mine did this effectively with a client with whom she'd had an uneven relationship. The client seemed strained during a conversation and followed up shortly after that with a terse e-mail: "I want to talk about the invoice." She phoned the client promptly and began with, "Here's a bit of good news," and then told him about progress on a key project. That said, she flowed into, "I know you want to talk about the work." By doing that, she put herself in charge of the conversation and in a position to address the client's pain and what she could continue to do to elimi-nate it. The client paid the invoice on schedule.

Sometimes you want to use the other person's words, and sometimes you want to avoid them completely, as in the previous scenario. It depends on what puts you in the driver's seat. Flip the scenario around, with the client's e-mail saying, "I want to talk about the project." You would want to set up the conversation by saying, "I'd like to report on project re-sults, how the project has evolved, and what results will come in the next phase of the project." Avoid the subject and you might as well shred the contract.

In general, people are conditioned to respond to that kind of leadership by jumping into your conversational stream.

Establish Rapport

In Chapter 2, I noted the ingredients of rapport (namely access sense and information sorting styles). In an interro-gation, I'm as likely to want to establish a negative rapport as I am a positive one—but it's still rapport. In other words, I'll work with what I've determined are his access sense and sorting style so that I can talk to him in his own terms, even if it is in a negative way. In your efforts to extract information from someone you know or from a business associate, the rapport you want is most likely positive.

Lots of signals can let you know if a person is visual. The fact that she dresses meticulously and accessorizes well. The fact that his office reflects an appreciation for art and a sense of color. It's a little harder to detect an auditory person; I'm one of them. One possible indication that the person tends to look sideways—toward the ears— in processing information. I have another theory: big ears. I'm not the only big-eared guy I know who falls in the auditory category. Another hint is a decided love of music. If your source has woofers and tweeters perfectly positioned in his office, then he may well be auditory. The hardest type of all to peg is kinesthetic. You might conclude that a person is kinesthetic if she has athletic hobbies, wears comfortable clothes, and says things such as, "I feel good about that" when a visual person might say, "I see how that could work well."

Pay close attention to the sorting styles, too. I know of many cases in which a contract was derailed by the conflict between a detail-oriented client and a big-picture consultant, or a sequential boss and a random employee. I am friends with a couple that has contrasting styles, almost from the beginning of the list to the end. But they know it and so they can often avoid misunderstandings. For example, when he calls from the road and asks, "What's new?" she knows that he expects not only highlights, but also details. If she asks the same question, he knows she only has the patience for the top one or two events of the day.

Enhance the rapport you build by matching your source's natural breathing cadence. When a person is not relaxed and comfortable, the pace and the depth of her breathing will differ from that natural style. If you mirror the cadence of her breathing in an easy state, she will feel comfortable with you and not know why.

Exercise

Listen to or watch an interview show, such as Fresh Air *on NPR,* The Ellen DeGeneres Show, *or* The Tonight Show. *Create profiles of the famous and near-famous people on the show based on your checklist of sorting styles and access senses.*

Use the Appropriate Approach(es)

What will make your source talk? The approaches I described earlier in this chapter should not pop up by accident. You know that in trying to close a big deal with a senior executive that a pride-and-ego down or fear-up mild approach is a mistake. Whittle down your options before the encounter, and then rank the merit of the remaining ones. This process gets faster and faster the more you go through it until it becomes almost automatic.

Ask Questions That Move You Down a Particular Path

Emotion and logic have to blend: You have to be logical with the questioning sequence while, at the same time, reinforcing your approach to keep the source in an emotional state.

For a business result, it may sound odd that I'm emphasizing the utility of emotion. But if you're selling a computer, trying to win a marketing contract, or asking your boss for a raise, what do you need to do? Keep reminding your target that you can ease her pain and increase her pleasure—these are emotional responses. The pain could be office inefficiency, bad public image, or the possibility of losing a senior staff member. The pleasure could be cost reductions, a higher profit margin, and stronger company loyalty. With practice, you'll know when to use direct, control, leading, and compound questions, and in the upcoming sections I'll give you specific guidance on using them.

Follow Your Source Leads

As a practical matter, interrogators keep lead sheets to jot down points in a conversation that merit scrutiny, but not at the moment. The same tactic for following up source leads works fine if you are in a meeting with several people and don't want to lose an idea worth pursuing. It would be odd, though, to use it in a conversation with your spouse that you hope will extract information, so I hope you have a short-term memory.

Looping back to a point is one of two ways to follow up source leads. The other is to exploit the information immediately and then move on to the next topic. The nature of the source lead will probably dictate which course to take.

Part of how you proceed depends on the person, too. If the person is sequence-driven, my immediate pursuit of a source lead might prove disconcerting to him. He has in his mind a series of events or concepts, and I could confuse him by asking a question that takes him off course. If, however, it's a person who's driven by the importance of an event, I'll probably want to follow up on the source lead immediately.

When you go headlong down a path for more facts, you do telegraph the value of that information. Ask yourself: Will it jeopardize the outcome of this encounter if he knows that piece is important to me? Looping back allows you to feign interest in various bits while your orchestrate your return to the key point.

Terminate

In a business meeting, it's the close: "Thanks for your time. I appreciate what we've accomplished." And then you review: "You've accomplished three of your objectives, I've accomplished three of mine...." In an interrogation, I'm likely to say, "I'm going to check what you told me for truth." I might even give the prisoner homework before I send him to his cell: "When I talk with you again, I want you to remember more about the number of weapons stockpiled."

Key points to remember throughout the process are:

◆ Keep up with leads. A lead can come at any time, whether or not you've asked a question. Follow up immediately or make a note so you don't lose the thought.

◆ Use active listening. Active listening contrasts with passive listening, or the act of letting sound hit you while you sit with your ears open, but not your mind. You invest your full range of senses in active listening so you can perceive the orchestration, choreography, and staging of someone's conversation—every part of voice, body, and presentation that conveys meaning.

◆ Keep eye contact. You will be able to mirror more effectively as well as spot deviations from the norm if you look at the person's face.

◆ Maintain your posture for whatever role you're playing. Unless you're playing the game of displaced expectations, you will need to be consistent in your presentation. Remember whom you brought to the dance!

◆ Transition to the termination phase. Wrap up with homework, no matter who the person is. It leaves her with a feeling that you're involved with her. In a business meeting, it could be, "I'll call your assistant tomorrow to get those numbers." In a personal confrontation, you might say, "I don't expect you to have an answer to that now. Let's both think about it and come back to that issue tomorrow."

Now, get ready to put the tools and the process together to get what you want in love and business relationships.

Section III:

Applying the Tools in Love

Chapter 7

Discovery

Understanding Othello

In preparing to write this section, I watched an hour of *The Oprah Winfrey Show* on a day that featured cheating husbands. First of all, if you haven't cleaned up your act after having an affair, don't go face to face with Oprah. Women in 119 countries will know you as a loser. One of the two men was in high limbic mode and repeatedly plunged his eyes down right. That statement of emotion could mean that he had extreme remorse about his transgression, or it could mean that he felt horrible about being discovered and, worse yet, about having his adultery broadcast on international television. Actually, it was probably a combination of both. He was in a weakened position to start with, and then he faced a formidable questioner: Oprah. I kept wondering if he had ever asked himself the question: "How much value does it add to my relationship to go on this show and face humiliation in front of millions of people?"

In exploring the two stories with the couples, Oprah took them back to the moment of discovery: How did they feel? What did they do? The woman whose husband had been a serial offender had lived in denial until denial seemed insane.

The woman whose husband kept leaking emotion with his eye movement admitted she yelled some "bad words" after receiving incontrovertible proof of his infidelity. Both could have found out about the affairs long before they did and taken steps to stop the hemorrhaging in their relationship, but they hadn't given in to suspicions and they weren't skilled in detecting lies.

Because you're reading this, you may be different from them. You have suspicions you can't dismiss. You just want to know how to prepare for the confrontations that will either confirm or refute them.

Your first challenge is that you must remain rational. In a relationship, you have preconceived notions and emotional expectations that you don't have in most business relationships. You also have rituals that drive your interaction; when your partner takes a step, it initiates a step on your part. In using the techniques described here, it's easier for you to distort what you see. Just as Othello concluded from circumstantial evidence that his innocent wife, Desdemona, had cheated on him, you could find your fears and suspicions shutting down your good judgment. The antidote is your cognitive mind.

Thoughts and actions that could help you move out of limbic mode and into cognitive thought relatively quickly include these three:

- Visualizing: You will see people who want to stop their tears move their eyes up—usually up left—in an effort to regain control. It's an instinctive maneuver that you can do consciously to access a memory that calms you down. You've probably noticed the converse of this action, as well—that is, people who want to wallow in emotion allow their eyes to move down and to the right.

- ◆ Making a list: This is analogous to counting
  sheep to get to sleep. A friend of mind said
  she calmed herself down in a very upsetting
  meeting by looking around the room and
  making a mental list of all the plastic surgery
  procedures that people in the room could
  have to make them more attractive. That particular exercise had the dual effect of making
  her feel more in control of the situation, not
  just of herself.
- ◆ Pinching yourself: I don't necessarily mean
  this literally, although you could try it. The
  point is to change your physical state with the
  intent that your mental state will follow.
  You've no doubt seen movies or daytime dra-
  mas in which someone is crying and then
  someone else comes along and slaps her. She
  stops crying and comes to her senses. Same
  thing there, but you find a way to do it to
  yourself. Rituals of all kinds condition your
  anxiety level.

Knowing someone very well provides inherent advantages to you in trying to spot a lie. You have a reason to be
curious, and maybe even suspicious, if your spouse deviates
from a long-standing routine for no apparent reason. If your
wife, who usually leaves the house with no make-up on because she goes to the gym before work, starts leaving at the
same early hour with her make-up on, you'd wonder why.
She's made a conscious decision to break with her pattern.
Alternatively, your husband might habitually put his keys in
a certain place when he comes home from work, go through
up the mail, change his clothes, and then pour himself a
drink. And then one day, you notice that his pattern has
changed. He plunks his keys down anywhere, avoids the
mail, and pours himself a drink before he changes his clothes.

Why would someone alter that sequence after 10 years of doing things the same way? His unconscious break with ritual is telling you something—you just don't know what. A mate's break with a cleansing ritual can hold a lot of significance, signaling a range of hidden issues, from ill health to infidelity. The everyday routines are the person's baseline; just as in interrogation, they indicate stress, not deception. Detecting deception is an art—and you have the tools!

Let's begin with the premise that you've noticed something odd. Don't try to baseline the person and extract information in the same session. You'll "do an Othello"— that is, ratchet up your own emotions and lose control. In this chapter, I'll focus on baselining.

I'll return to the scenario with Samantha and her husband in Chapter 5. There, she failed. Now, watch her when she's more agile with the baselining techniques, as well as her approaches and questioning strategy. Presume also that she used her skills well in the meeting with the prospect and closed the deal.

Scenario: Playing Lie Detector With a Spouse

Samantha came home from her successful meeting with the prospective client and picked up the mail. She made a mental note of the fact that her husband, Bill, had received a card from his ex-wife. It wasn't his birthday, nor any other special occasion. One thing popped into her head: a thank-you card. Bill had promised Samantha that he would stop sending money to his ex-wife for her college tuition. She believed that he had stopped until a few weeks ago, when he hedged on a conversation about buying a new house. Considering her next steps, Samantha figured she had three options:

1. Confront him.
2. Determine whether or not he's deceiving her, and then simply announce that she knows he's lying about something.
3. Maneuver him into a position where he has no choice except to tell the truth.

Option #1 didn't appeal to her because she didn't want to look like a fool if her guess was wrong. She also knew from her failed, previous marriage that confrontation could lead to a violent emotional outburst. Sure, Bill wasn't the same person as her ex, but she had those blow-ups etched in her memory.

Samantha opted to use her newly developed skills in lie detection to find out what Bill was really up to. I've provided the end of the story here using both remaining options so you can see how she could arrive at the same outcome in different ways.

Samantha Pursues Option #2

Shedding the persona of the in-charge executive, Samantha decided to be the attentive wife in her baselining conversation with Bill. After he came in the door and put his keys in the normal place, he did his second after-work ritual: He grabbed a snack, usually a handful of nuts or a hunk of cheese.

"How was your day," she began.

"Usual."

"What time did you get to work?"

"Eight."

After they finished the small talk, Samantha knew she needed to ask questions to see if Bill is a hard left or a hard right—something most people probably don't know about their spouses until they actually study their reactions.

Samantha began with a control question: "When is your nephew's soccer tournament again? Is it the weekend of the 18th or the 25th?" She saw him glance to the upper left to recall the date. "I thought I'd get him a present to celebrate the fact that his team made it into the finals. I know he wants that new Beck CD with that song—what the heck is it?" Again, another control question. She knows that Bill's favorite song on the Beck CD is "Black Tambourine." She watched his eyes go directly left as the song ran through his head. Throughout the evening they just continued to chat, not even mentioning the touchy subject, and Samantha mentally recorded what Bill did with his eyes and body in responding to different types of questions. She even had a little extra fun by asking him to speculate what the skinny girl down the street would look like with breast implants. But no matter what they discussed, there was no way he would have known that this conversation was unlike any other they had ever had.

Having baselined him, the next day she began to collect information. She called his office at 8:30 in the morning just to talk about something, and he wasn't there. Not thinking anything of it, she drove past his office on her way to work and saw that his car wasn't in the parking lot. A bit farther down the road, she saw it parked in front of a motel. "Whoa! This isn't what I expected!" Trying to remain calm, she drove to her office. As she was picking up a latte from the coffee shop, she saw her brother-in-law Bob's next-door neighbor.

"Hey, Samantha. Saw your husband this morning when he dropped the car off for Bob. Nice guy! I can't believe how many times he's helped out that brother of his. Probably be cheaper if he just bought him a new car."

Samantha's blood pressure quickly went back to normal. She thought: "So, it's Bill's brother who's the bad boy.

Well, that still gives me some interesting stuff to play with for my purposes."

And then the neighbor added, "Oh, and tell Bill I really am sorry I couldn't join his foursome this morning."

"He's playing golf!"

"Oops. Pretend I never said that, okay?"

Samantha now got some real amusement out of Bill's situation. He definitely wanted to hide at least one thing from her, and she was going to leverage that to find out what she really wanted to know.

Later that evening, Samantha greeted Bill in the usual way, except that the role she brought to the dance was a sexy girlfriend, not the attentive wife. "How was your day, dear?"

"Usual."

"What time did you get to work?"

"Eight."

"Funny. I called you around 8:30 to see if you wanted to go to a movie tonight and you weren't around." At that, she saw him fidget. "Did you have a meeting this morning?" she asked innocently.

"I got together with a couple of the guys at the office to go over some things."

In her mind, Samantha silently congratulated him, "Nice job of conditioning that question, dude!" Out loud, she said, "Are you feeling okay? You look at little red in the face." She knew darned well that he'd gotten some sun on the golf course.

"I'm fine. Oh, look, I don't want to lie to you, baby. I played golf this morning."

"Don't worry about it," she cooed. "Everyone needs a break now and then. It's not like you're having an affair or something. Why would you ever think you couldn't tell me something you did?"

With that, Samantha saw Bill's eyes to down right. She soon eased into a conversation about buying the new house and saw his eyes go down right again. He was growing emotional and weak. A simple "What's wrong, honey?" finally got him to admit that he was sending money to his ex-wife for her college tuition.

Samantha Pursues Option #3

(In this scenario, Samantha learned everything about the car and Bill's whereabouts in exactly the same way, but she decided to use them in a different way.)

Later that evening, Samantha greeted Bill in the usual way, except that the role she brought to the dance was the senior executive, not the attentive wife or sexy girlfriend. "How was your day?"

"Usual."

"What time did you get to work?"

"Eight."

"Funny. I called you around 8:30 to ask for your opinion on a project and you weren't around." At that, she saw him fidget. "Did you have a meeting this morning?"

"I got together with a couple of the guys at the office to go over some things."

She silently congratulated him on conditioning the question. Out loud, she said, "You look at little red in the face. Sure you weren't out playing golf?"

"Look, you got me. I played a quick nine with Ted and Bill from the office."

"Who drove?"

"What do you mean?"

"When I passed the Comfy Motel on my way to the office, I saw your car there so you couldn't have driven."

Samantha saw that he looked stricken—eyebrows arched in surprise, jaw tight, arms back. Bill leaked emotion all over the place. Before he even had a chance to tell her about loaning the car to his brother, she continued, "And I saw that your ex-wife sent you a card yesterday. Do you think I'm stupid? If she's going to send you love notes about your little affair, the least she could do is use e-mail!" With that, Samantha saw Bill's eyes to down right and then look straight at her.

"No, I loaned my car to my brother, and I have no idea why it was at the motel! And that note, it was a thank-you note for sending her money for college!" Samantha applauded her skillful use of minimalizing.

"Oh, really? I believe you, Bill. I couldn't believe you would cheat on me. Now let's talk about that money...."

Chapter 8

Extract
the Truth

In Chapter 4, we explored the concept of Semper Gumbi and that fact that rigid people can be knocked off center easily. Here's the extreme downside in a personal relationship: You may try to apply the techniques in this book within the context of your marriage or other serious love affair. If the other person involved has those characteristics of predictability with clothing, for example, and if that person invests emotionally in controlling his or her environment, you could see some nasty behavior result from a disruption of those externals. That's natural. Your spouse or partner would be resorting to a self-preservation response. You need to know your source, but you also need to heed your context. Most likely, you won't get the information or results you want by driving your spouse or partner into a violent rage. Unlike dealing with a prisoner of war, your situation is very complex. What you do affects not only the other person in the relationship, but also the relationship itself. You also don't want to debut an entirely new role for your interrogation dance. If you do, where does that role live when the interchange is over?

Nevertheless, you do have to think as the interrogator in order to use the tools of the interrogator. Primarily, stay focused on the fact that you want to extract the truth, not a confession. If all you want is a confession, all you need are barbaric tools.

Planning and Preparation

Change the Scenery

Emotions can arise from nowhere due to past experiences, ritual, trappings, and myriad other things. In order be methodical in getting your spouse to tell you the truth, you'll benefit from disconnecting yourself from some of these elements.

Love relationships create a very sophisticated dance. Most involve some sort of contract—written or unwritten—that establishes entitlements. How many of these contracts carry undeclared expectations? Are they understood? Over time, you have established give-and-take rituals for both the entitlements and the expectations. This evolution has created powerful rituals around food, sex, and sleep, among other things. This relationship has also created powerful trappings associated with the expectations. The main concept is that this relationship makes it very difficult to carry out an interrogation-like exercise. Beware.

To accomplish the exercise, the first thing to do is change the scenery. Go somewhere where there is little or no emotional connotation or connection to your trappings or rituals. This does a couple of things:

- It reduces the likelihood of baggage associated with the process.
- It separates the usual you from the you in the exercise.

Do Your Homework

Bluffing is a bad idea. Glossing over a fact will come back to haunt you. Know dates, times, places, and numbers. If you cannot know all details, do enough research to know where the blanks exist, but do not fill them in. Using the We Know All approach with enough detail is more likely to work than trying to fill in the blanks yourself.

Baseline

You know there are rituals that occur within the confines of the relationship, but these can skew your data when you baseline the one you love. Your best opportunity to baseline will be when your spouse or partner is with other acquaintances. Then compare this baseline to the one for your daily interactions. Everyone knows that most people are different in dealing with people outside the immediate family, and this is due to the intimate relationships and the rituals established. Baseline on absolutes, such as pitching statistics or how many miles it is to the outlet mall. Ask questions that do not include any past history or emotion.

Roles

Do you want to appeal to your high school sweetheart, the successful businessman, or the weekend athlete? Do you want to be the prom queen, the incisive journalist, or the mother? Decide and stick to it. Do not allow rituals to take you off path.

Questioning

Prepare to ask new questions, but in your own voice. You do not want to suddenly sound as I do—that would probably be a shocker to your spouse—so choose a style that fits her demeanor and yet allows little wiggle room.

Ask questions that either get useful answers or that steer the conversation toward the information you seek.

Be cognizant of signals and rituals, and be careful how you use the signals of the relationship because the other person is attuned to reading that specific body language as much as you are attuned to hers. When she tells you she was at work all day and you tilt your head, she will recognize the hint of disbelief . You may blow your entire approach and line of questioning.

Sometimes confrontation works well. People can't hide surprise. The eyebrows go up, and the eyes get big. At that point, the surprised person has to take the next step, whether it's invent a story really fast, tell the truth, go speechless, cry, or have some other significant reaction. Taking the direct-question approach if you suspect a lie should extract the truth fairly quickly. How many details can a person who's just invented a story possibly come up with? You'll see if they're rehearsed, and the story will fall apart if they're not.

Direct confrontation does not have to be mean. Here's how I would do it with a prisoner while I'm playing the role of the nice guy, relying primarily on a futility approach: "Let's not be stupid about this. You're in captivity. You're here for a reason: We don't like your government. Let's figure this out. We're a superpower and we're winning. Let's make your life pleasant. Close down this battle. Get you back home to see your family. Let's get this done."

You can use the same structure with your cheating spouse: "I know your car was at the motel because I saw it. I called your office when I saw just to be sure. You weren't there. Let's figure this out. Just admit it and we can move on from there. Let's get this part of the battle over with so we sort out how to make peace."

What if you bluffed? You had the bit about the car correct, but you didn't call the office. Your spouse says,

"I loaned my car to Billy and, yes, I was in the office in front of my computer working on the monthly sales report. Even if you called when I was in the bathroom, my phone would have displayed your number as a missed call." Well, now you look like a fool, but at least were you a calm, logical fool.

Locking into your spouse's method of sorting information is probably your best offensive and defensive maneuver. If your spouse or partner is lying to you, it's likely that person will try hard to think the way you think. If you're punctual (time-driven), she will try to recount details of the lie in terms of time: "I was at the office at 10:30 and then went to lunch at 11:45." This may not even be a conscious effort. But let's say that the liar is a time-driven person and you are sequence-driven. The fact that she was at her office at 10:30 is not as relevant as what happened before and what happened after. When you ask about that, you may find chinks in the story.

Whether you use confrontation or an indirect approach, as your spouse or partner responds, you may think, "We've been here before." You have to be careful not to overlay your emotions from a past experience. People get in cycles of arguments because of that: "This feels like last time you lied to me!" You've got to step back and, even though the trappings are the same, analyze the current conversation as a separate event. Avoid emotional déjà vu—that is, overlaying past experiences on the current situation.

As you ask control questions and repeat questions that exploit information, do not accuse. Hate the sin, not the sinner. Get ready to talk about the contract and your entitlements.

Chapter 9

Change the
Way You Fight

The skill of arguing is an integral part of interrogation. In their interrogation school, the Brits start off their new students with a mint between two of them. The two newbies have to argue logically about who should get the mint first. Whoever wins, gets the mint. It might go similar to this:

"Why should you get the mint?"

"I just had lunch. I have garlic breath and I think you will benefit if I get the mint."

One beautiful blonde used a classic incentive approach when she leaned across the table and offered the male interrogator something he wanted a lot more than the mint. And she would need it to freshen her breath.

In interrogation, arguing is that back-and-forth exchange in which the prisoner thinks he actually has a shot at establishing intellectual dignity or at humiliating his captor. But the interrogator remains in cognitive thought, even though she might seem emotional, whereas the prisoner sinks deeper and deeper into limbic mode. One person assumes clear control as the other's position gets weaker and weaker. By giving you specific guidance on how to argue, I'm just showing you how to use the tools we've already covered to do one of three things:

1. Argue artfully to improve your relationship.
2. Win at all costs.
3. Send an argument off the tracks.

First, I'll offer two reasons why people supposedly in love snarl at each other. One is displaced emotion and another is displaced expectations.

You can't afford to call your boss or co-worker a jerk, so you repress the emotion at work. This can be dangerous when you come home because a small thing might release rage that's way out of proportion to the event. You get in a nasty fight with your spouse over something your boss did. In other words, you've displaced your emotion.

Displaced expectations have to do with your spouse or partner violating your emotions or your possessions. Basically, he or she has disturbed something that you think belongs to you. That could mean an intangible such as entitlements in the relationship—fidelity, love, public displays of affection, a clean house, silence, respect, conversation, and so on. That could also mean something tangible, such as your stuff. Whether the person has taken you for granted, undervalued your expertise, or trashed your possessions, the physiological effect is the same: You ramp up. You don't take time to prepare for that kind of argument— you just explode. You become the little red-headed boy that everybody mocks, or the pigeon-toed geek who kids don't pick for their team, or the girl with thick glasses who never looks pretty. You're at your weakest at that moment; you feel violated and angry.

Ground Rules for Productive Fights

The starting point for effective arguing is cognitive thought. A lot of times, during or after a heated argument, one or both parties will say, "I didn't mean to say that." Take that at face value. When people are in limbic mode, they will say things that merit the label "irrational." Arguing productively is about saying exactly what you mean. What I'm trying to give you are guidelines for remaining in cognitive thought—the way interrogators must—so that arguing becomes debate. You want to make sense, have a point, and conclude effectively.

Rule #1

Keep the argument focused on a subject, not a person. When an argument degrades to a personal attack, you push buttons that make it extremely difficult to back out of limbic mode and return to your primate brain. You want to reduce the stress that's inherent in a confrontation to have a good shot at keeping yourself and the other person in cognitive thought.

A man doesn't necessarily realize that criticizing his wife's driving is criticizing her. Almost invariably, it comes across as a stab at the woman's competence. Conversely, a woman might say some harsh words about the way her husband feeds the kids. It may sound no different from an accusation that he's careless. Maybe your fundamental issues with each do relate to competence and carelessness, but addressing them in an obtuse way can be likened to treating a broken leg by bandaging your nose. Talk directly about the elephant in the living room.

Watch for the drift away from the incident and toward the personal attack and stop it cold:

"No wonder you dented the fender—you're mindless when you drive!"

"We've got to get through this sanely. If you have an issue with me, let's talk about me, but this car wreck is not me. This is not about me being incompetent. This is not about me being stupid. This is about a damaged car we need to discuss."

Rule #2

Only debate things you know about. When you argue about things you know nothing about and continually lose, you establish a harmful pattern. You're also much more likely to get emotional in discussing topics that shouldn't affect you emotionally. Even if you lose these arguments 50 percent of the time, you still establish a bad pattern of you coming across as ignorant and belligerent. If you only argue when you have solid facts in your head, then you win. And when you realize your logic or memory can't hold up to a challenge, back off discreetly—say something such as "that's interesting"—or ask a question that takes you in a direction you can handle.

Rule #3

When someone does start to yell, go silent. Do not respond until the yelling stops. Spend the time concentrating to pull yourself back from emotion and into your prefrontal cortex. If you yell back, the other person feels justified in yelling and you spiral downward into joint insanity.

Rule #4

Learn to speak the same language. Whether it is because you are a different sex, different Myers-Briggs type, different culture, or different learning mode, or some other difference, no two people are going to have identical communication styles. If we define communication as two or more people using a common system of symbols to exchange ideas, you can quickly see where the gap is: common. This lesson is important whether you want to win at all costs or argue for a better relationship. If you are an SJ personality type who values security and time lines and you marry an NF, expect some setbacks. The classic Archie/Edith get-to-the-point argument will consistently raise its head in a household composed of an event-sorter and a time-sorter. Whether you want to accommodate for a better relationship or simply dominate arguments, this is the most powerful thing to learn.

How to Win Just to Win

If your aim is simply to win, then use questions to redirect the argument. Often, the quickest way to redirect is to turn the question back on the questioner:

> "How could you let Johnny go to a party like that?"

> "Why would you abdicate all your parental responsibility to me?"

The most effective path is to redirect the argument so that the other person's greatest faults receive the spotlight. Your husband begins the conversation berating you about getting into a fender bender. You quickly make his shortcomings the center of attention. Did his carelessness ever lead to a worse accident? Was he negligent in maintaining the car? How many tickets has he gotten that have driven your insurance rates up? This is a low, dark, mean way to win, but you will win. He surely won't want to talk about his faults—nobody does; he wants to talk about yours. Of course, when you choose to take this tack with an argument, you value winning more than the relationship.

A less-confrontational version of redirecting an exchange is herding the conversation as a way of forcing the person out of cognitive thought and into reactionary thought. I call it herding because I've watched my dogs herd animals on the farm. The dogs don't constantly guide the cattle, for example. They do course corrections, as a pilot does. They move the other animals in a direction and then let them move freely. When the dogs get to a point where they know the herd should turn, then they drive them in that direction. Doing this in a conversation, can allow you to "win"—that is, outscore logic points. In the course of maneuvering this way and that—a course of your design—the other person might utter something that undermines his argument. Do what the media does all the time: Quote him out of context. The pattern goes this way: Logical conversation; diversion that arouses some emotion, thereby reducing his ability to argue logically; digging out words or ideas that serve your purposes; getting what you want.

When we were doing a show with volunteer prisoners for Channel 4 in England, I pegged a bright 22-year-old Pakistani native as a terrorist suspect. I asked him about organizing terrorists and he said something along the lines of, "I can't possibly have done that. I'm a kid. I don't have those organizational skills." I let him pass with that at the time and decided to use it later. I started asking him about his loyalties. He described himself as a Muslim and a Brit. I asked which is more important, and he said Islam. I kept pushing: Which is more important, Britain or Pakistan? He said he belonged to both, so he couldn't make a choice. How would you decide if they went to war with each other—which one you would fight for? "I'll go with the one that's more just," he said. And then I used his words against him: "Just? You arrogant son of a bitch! You're willing to put yourself on a par with God to determine what's just, but you're just a kid who can't even organize a handful of people?" That upset him, so he came back with a statement that he'd rely on someone he trusted to tell him. At that point, I had him.

If we had continued a logical conversation we never would have gotten to that breaking point. The ploy strained his ability to think, to pull from memory, so that all he could do was react. As he saw, it's hard to argue with your own words. And to the target of the tactic, it doesn't even feel as though he was quoted out of context; it feels as though it's the same context because it's the same argument.

Herding a conversation may sound hard, but you've probably done this naturally many times. The technique involves dropping source leads when you don't want to talk about something so that you guide the conversation in a different direction. In this instance, the conversation involves a confrontational aspect and the technique is a tool to end the dispute with the upper hand. You lose, of course, if your "opponent" figures out the game plan.

One tactic interrogators use to shove prisoners into an extreme limbic state is to use prejudice and mockery. When I was a kid, people made fun of me for my red hair and big ears. As an adult, I'd better be well past the point when a red-headed joke or a big-eared joke upsets me. Those kinds of jibes can actually work with grown men and women, though, because they affect a very soft spot in them. To some people, ridiculing them for a slight deformity or the color of their skin is nonsense that evaporates as soon as it hits their ears. To other people, "them's fightin' words," and a huge wave of emotion begins to rush over them. They can't help it because they aren't practiced in keeping the emotion at bay. One of your defenses in arguing has got to be to ignore every taunt and every expletive as if the person spewing them just barked or chirped or made some other sound that means nothing to the human ear.

Derailing an Argument

Control questions, repeat questions, vague questions—
these are all tools to stop a situation where it is one person
attacking and one person defending. You want to derail
an argument because you don't care about winning and
you don't think anything productive can come out of con-
tinuing it. A good time to derail an argument is when you've
both had too much to drink.

Your main tactic is sidetracking if you want to move
completely away from a hot topic or a point that causes
discomfort. Pick up on a comment that allows you to take
a fork in the road and go with it. Let's say you're an envi-
ronmentalist who mentions that you had a Mustang before you realized you could get better gas mileage with a
Honda Civic and you are hot on the point of pollution,
and civic responsibility, and—

"Mustang? I didn't know you had a Mustang. What
year was it?"

"2002."

"I had a '68. It was piece of crap. The windows were
busted out of it. I had to go and buy windows. That wasn't
the worst part. The windows were easy to find, but the
gaskets were impossible. So I ended up having to use this
glue-in window, and then I got rust around it. It took me
two years to get the rust out of it, and then I wrecked the
damned thing."

To be polite, you'll probably say something in response
to my comment, and when I respond, I'll take you off topic
even further. And to make this tactic work well, don't say
anything that will stimulate circulate logic and take you
back on the original topic.

Reverse the perspective. What if you were the one
making the point and someone took you off course? One
way that's done is to fixate on a word or concept such

as "gasket." You could go the ignorant route and interrupt me with: "What's a gasket?" And when I finish answering, you simply move back to your point. Or you could
venture, "Not a problem anymore. Ebay has everything
for old cars." And then you return to your point.

Chapter 10

Are You in Love or Captivity?

Shock of Capture

The first time you hear, and perhaps feel, the abuse of your spouse, that's the shock of capture. How could you possibly stay rational? This is the emotional equivalent of having a hood thrown over your head and your arms and legs bound by cord in the middle of the night. You are the equivalent of the garage-band guitarist/soldier walking through the woods on patrol not expecting the ambush. Your mind has no mailbox to store the data of the overwhelming new experience.

The reasons for getting into a relationship vary according to our needs and desires, but one factor people have in common is that they don't get in a relationship to fail. After the shock of capture, the brain scrambles to come to life and find reasons why this incident is not a sign of failure. It's just a misunderstanding—a problem that can be fixed tomorrow.

Displaced expectations—the walking-on-eggshells feeling—figures prominently in this scenario. The captor constantly changes expectation to establish the role of being perfect. Interrogators are professional anxiety brokers; the only difference between them and abusive husbands and wives is the word *professional*. The abusive spouse sets up unrealistic expectations and then, through the companion treatments of kindness and manipulation, creates unease, so the person cannot know what to expect next. Entitlements in the relationship, such as honesty and the expectation that well-intended gestures will not earn physical or emotional torture, are violated. Everyone in a personal relationship has those rights.

Everyone in an interrogation relationship does not have those rights, however, and that is why the abused and abuser have so much in common with the prisoner and the captor. The captive's primary concern—self-preservation—causes one question to guide virtually every action: "Am I doing the right thing or the wrong thing?" Just as in the prisoner-guard relationship, only the captor can answer the question. Just as the prisoner who was captured and moved to the rear was, the abused person is now dependent on new inputs to define the unknown role. The abused person gives feedback to the abuser as the prisoner does to the guard.

Say you're in the most extreme version of the situation from the physical perspective. Your spouse slaps you around, beats you, and finds other insidious ways to make you physically uncomfortable. You are forced into limbic mode; your amygdala goes into overdrive, so you constantly show the effects of negative emotion. That sustained state will grind down your health, your looks, and your mind. You will figuratively, and perhaps literally, stumble through life in confusion over what's right and what's wrong.

Say you're in an extreme version of the situation from a mental and emotional perspective. You may not display the physical traits of abuse, but you are still similar to the prisoner of war, captured on the battlefield, and marched through the gates of hell and into an enemy compound. As he does, you constantly hear, in some form, "You idiot.

You moron. You can't meet my standards—it's impossible." Eventually, that starts to take its toll and you feel you have no value.

In both cases, when you slump into a perception that you're worthless, your resistance to any kind of pressure starts to drop. You have the trappings of a victim, the rituals of a victim, and so you easily fill the role of a victim. It's how you adapt to the situation. You give to the "guard"—that is, your spouse—ultimate power to dictate how and when you will accommodate him. He gets you to that point because he engages in a systematic removal of your identity. Invariably, a key element of this phenomenon is cloistering the victim—separation from family and friends. You begin to internalize every word because you don't have the input from family and friends about your wit, charm, looks, and value. When you are sequestered, just as the prisoner does, you start to see everything in black and white. If you burn dinner you must be an incompetent cook. A car accident and burned dinner mean you can't do anything right. The dance that is your daily life and the role you fill in it spins out of control. The final stage is that everything becomes personal. An attack on one of your children might even be a welcome relief; you think, "At least it's not me this time."

As a prisoner of war does, you start to think that your environment dominated by a guard is normal. When it gets incrementally worse, you won't even notice it. This is the human version of that myth about frogs: Put a frog in a pot of hot water and it will jump out. Put it in cold water and turn up the temperature, and it will not notice the change and boil to death. This isn't true, by the way, so act as a real frog does and jump as the temperature rises!

How did you get to be the victim and what can you do about it?

For discussion purposes, let's say you got A's in school, were co-captain of the cheerleading squad, and graduated *cum laude* with a degree in chemistry. Your parents held you up as the model child for your younger brother, an overweight kid who struggled with studies. To you, success seemed inevitable. You married a handsome lawyer, had two children, and, by the age of 30, your life was hell. He never beat you, but you spent every day in terror of his verbal abuse, his relentless criticism of your clothes, your cooking, your cellulite. You kept thinking that he only said those things to help you, to improve you. Of course he loves you; otherwise he wouldn't bother. It goes on and on until death do you part. What happened?

Here's a scenario that I saw many times with prisoners: Your little box inside contains pride of accomplishment/fear of failure. I glean that fact by talking with you about your achievements and I see the pain in your face and body when you talk about a failure, such as being captured. I do simple things centered on your fear of failure to manipulate you. I put two food tins in front of you and say, "Pick one. That's your meal today." You pick one and it's empty. "Oops. Too bad you chose the wrong one." Of course, both tins were empty. He will get dinner anyway (it's illegal to withhold food from a prisoner), but I still proved he is a failure by giving him dinner out of pity. I show how great and magnanimous I am; after all, I am the model. In one incident after another, I convince you, "You're wrong. I'm right." Keep in mind that human beings need interaction. But if the only human interaction you have is with me, a man skilled in eroding your self-esteem, your need is being met in a sick way that ultimately destroys that drive at the core of your being. I convince you that the only way to feel worthwhile again is be compliant. You begin to believe me;

this is *Stockholm Syndrome*. Do what I want and tell me what I need to know, and you rise up to full personhood again.

The husband in the scenario isn't necessarily persecuting you deliberately, although some spouses do know exactly what to do to wield power over their mate. Regardless of his motivation or level of consciousness about it, however, you are in captivity.

Now add a complication: You have an affair with your son's teacher. He often compliments you on raising such an outstanding student and polite kid. He appreciates that you're always on time for parent-teacher conferences. He might be good-looking, but his profound appeal is the way he honors what's in your little box: pride of accomplishment/fear of failure.

In essence, this is no different from my sending in the "good cop" after I tear you down in an interrogation. In comes a soft-spoken colleague who woos you: "Someone as brilliant as you must know this...."

Escape From Captivity

There are logical ways to extricate yourself from a captive relationship, and there are bizarre ways. Unfortunately, the latter sometimes seem much easier. A friend's neighbor felt abused by her husband, so she reported him to the police for molesting their young children. In her mind, that lie of commission was justified. Her mind told her that self-preservation had to take precedence over everything else and that this ploy would exploit the law to keep him away from her home.

I cannot tell you how to get out of your abusive relationship, but I can tell you that external input is absolutely essential. You can't rely on your own judgment of

your situation for accuracy. Get help. I can give you techniques to counter a person who makes you feel as though
you're a captive in an attempt to help you restore some
cognitive thought. They are predicated on the notion that
you are aware that the person has tried, consciously or
unconsciously, to condition you to accept him as an supreme authority figure and that you must take deliberate
steps to change that. Begin by trying to change the ground
rules about arguing, criticism, and even small talk.

- As I described in Chapter 9, only argue about
  things you know about. Right about now, a
  hoard of psychologists and marriage counse-
  lors want my head for telling you how to argue
  with an abusive spouse. In response, I can only
  say that this is a book on using interrogation
  techniques to probe, defend, survive, and
  thrive. I leave the therapy to the therapists.

- Don't get defensive. In filming The History
  Channel's *We Can Make You Talk*, one of the
  prisoners was a stunning American woman
  of Sri Lankan heritage. In a pride-down approach, which is what the bad husband in the
  scenario is running, one of the male interrogators mocked her "big, birthing hips." Staring right into his eyes, she told him she was
  glad to have birthing hips because she wanted
  to have children someday.

- Learn to derail a discussion that's heating up.
  This is a common cocktail party technique
  that also can help avert an argument at home.
  You hear yourself getting sucked into a conversation about a controversial political
  speech, so you pick up a single word or phrase
  and run in a different direction with it: "My
  cousin watched that speech the day before

she gave birth to twin girls." With this one, you do run the risk of eliciting a criticism about "how you can't follow a logical train of thought" or something else that sounds to be "you're too stupid to have a conversation." Be prepared for that and let it serve as a reminder that you should seek the help of a therapist immediately.

Section IV:

Applying the Tools to Business

Chapter 11

Getting the Upper Hand in a Meeting

The guidance I provide in this chapter focuses on meetings with a purpose, just as every "meeting" I have had with a prisoner has a purpose. Even so, this chapter may also help you introduce purpose into those regular staff meetings that occur regardless of whether or not anyone has a point to make.

Planning and Preparation

Most people I meet in a business environment have never done what I'm about to tell you to do: Prior to your initial meeting with someone, exploit all source documents available to you. Read articles, online references, and whatever else you can find to know as much as possible about the company and the person or people with whom you'll be meeting. How do I know that most people don't do this? They blather on about themselves and ask superficial questions about me. If they had done the tiniest bit of research, they would know that the reason I'm a certain type of business consultant is that I have interrogation expertise. They wouldn't make fools of themselves asking irrelevant or vague questions.

Much of what you learn about your subject(s) may never come up in conversation but, as you will see when I go into approaches, your in-depth knowledge can affect how you go about getting your desired outcome.

Ask questions of people ancillary to your main contact after you do your document research. These would be people you know have dealt with her in the past or see her now through business or social connections. Keep in mind that it's the nature of people to hold back a little piece of information when questioned about something. They may not even be conscious of it, but asking, "What else can you tell me about her?" will often pull out pertinent details.

Interrogators collect information from the people around the prisoners—namely, guards. The business equivalents of guards are co-workers. If you have access to one of them—a receptionist, for example—in casual conversation you can ask questions that will make your first meeting with the person go more smoothly. "I had a quick question before our meeting tomorrow. Can he take a call right now?" "No, he's in a meeting for the next 30 minutes." "He sounds like a busy guy. Does he travel a lot, too?" Ancillary people will give you more information that the primary source will give you about himself.

You ask these questions because you want insights into the person's various roles, as well a sense of her priorities and how she does business. Again, I'll go into this in the approaches section.

Other critical elements of preparation include:

- Brief anyone thoroughly that you take into a meeting. Make sure you don't step on each other and that everyone knows who sets the pace, takes the tough questions, and handles the termination. Have signals worked out about who takes the next part of a question, who buys lunch, or whatever issues might arise.

- Have your props ready. Don't dig through your computer bag to find a chart and don't spend time rummaging through your computer files to find a document you need.

- Match your uniform to your approach. Something in your head has to buy into your role completely, so choosing the right costume makes a big difference. You can come across as overbearing, deferential, professional, sexy, childlike, sloppy, and any number of other types depending on what you wear—from head to toe.

Selecting the Approach

Elements to consider in determining the approach you use in a business situation mirror those I've used with prisoners. With each factor, consider what approaches automatically fall off the list of possibilities. For any business situation, of course, *fear-up harsh* will not apply. *Fear-up mild* rarely is appropriate, and certainly never with someone you need to adopt a solicitous stance with. The exception to this is when you detect the pain of a prospect and you know you have the solution. You may want to magnify the impact of the problem before showing him that, for a fee, you can stitch that cut. *Establish identity* and the *rapid-fire approach* also don't fit well into the business environment, so you're left with these eight: *direct, incentive, emotional, fear down, pride and ego, futility, repetition,* and *silence*. Remember that the approach comes late in the game, after you set up everything else. Understanding the person's basic style, type, position, and needs will enable you to find his pain. You want to get to a point where he has two options: one that involves you solving his problem and another in which he continues to suffer alone. Approaches are levers that help create or magnify the wound you will suture—for a fee.

Going into the meeting, you should have a grasp of the following:

- Mental and physical state: A CEO whose company's stock price is up and has just been featured in *Forbes* will have one mental state. The CEO of a company on the slide will probably feel more desperate and be consumed with problem-solving. The mental states may affect the person's physical comfort, with the latter creating a greater need to have reassuring trappings around him. Age and experience could mitigate that need, however.

- Age and experience: How long has this person been in his position? How long has she been in a comparable position? An executive who has held several top spots with companies may not be shaken by a plummeting stock price. In fact, if she's a turnaround expert, she might be right where she wants to be, ready to explode with genius and power. Even if she's not a turnaround expert, long-term experience leading a company with problems could have caused her to adapt to the stress, just as a longtime prisoners develop mechanisms to become less sensitive to their captivity.

- Background: Did this person build the company from the ground up, or did he rise through the ranks of other companies and then assume leadership in a new environment? Did he gain a foothold in the upper echelons of corporate power because of a mentor, or a brilliant deal? The contrast here is between someone who has enormous confidence and pride and someone who may still be somewhat tentative about where he is in the corporate world.

+ Length of approach: Do you have an hour with the person or an afternoon? Is this someone you will see day after day for a period of time? If you are unsure, then he has established control and you are not the interrogator, you are the prisoner.

Ground Rules for a Meeting

How many times have you sat in a meeting and wondered if the intent was to prevent progress, delay action, muddy the agenda, or stroke someone's ego? Sounds similar to what a savvy prisoner would do in a meeting with an interrogator. Don't let anyone undermine your meeting in that way. Set up some rules for yourself and for anyone who has to be responsive to you.

At the very beginning, verbally tell everyone the following, regardless of whether or not it's written in a formal notice or e-mail:

+ Agenda.
+ Amount of time for the agenda.
+ How to go from item to item on the agenda (presentations in succession, an "organic" approach guided by discussion, and so on).
+ Problems or tough issues that will be discussed.
+ Roles that everyone will play (subject matter expert, parliamentarian, consultant, recording secretary).
+ Desired outcome.

Remember that authority is given most of the time, not taken. In other words, by the way other people respond to you, they give you authority. When you make it clear, even in a meeting of your peers, that you have a plan to move the meeting forward, people often will be inclined to cede authority to you.

Even in a meeting between two people, in which you are the one making a pitch to a decision-maker, you can use the same model. You'd probably handle it with more subtlety, though:

◆ Agenda: "Thank you for seeing me to discuss the contract."

◆ Amount of time for the agenda: "We agreed to 40 minutes. Is that still valid?" Use words that have meaning and sound as though they're an obligation.

◆ How to go from item to item on the agenda: "I have a number of questions prepared. Are you okay with starting like that?"

◆ Ask the person for input to the agenda to add buy-in to your list. It makes the list hers as well.

◆ Problems or tough issues that will be discussed: "Here are the key issues I'd like to cover with you.... Is there anything you need to add to that?"

◆ Roles that everyone will play: You decide before you go into the meeting if you are bringing the dancer who will lead or the dancer who will follow, the one who has the innovative moves or the one who follows the steps of the dance as if they were painted on the floor. You also decide before you go into the meeting with whom you want to dance, and pay attention to the role the other person is putting out front.

♦ Desired outcome: "What I hope to do is address all your concerns and give you straight answers to questions so that you can get what you want out of this contract."

Matching Location to Objective

You've no doubt heard the three most important considerations in real estate: location, location, location. The location of the "real estate" you stake out in a meeting is important, too, as is the size of your territory.

Position at a table matters. If it didn't, why would a father traditionally sit at the head of the table? Why would the president of a board of directors sit at the head table? It does matter. Territory is a primordial drive for humans, as it is for any primate.

When you take a seat at a meeting, stake out territory that helps you make the right statement. That does not mean you should set up your laptop at the end, if you are not the one running the meeting. In fact, in a small meeting with client, you will very likely want that person to feel honored by having the slot at the head of the table.

When people arrive at a meeting and begin to spread out their papers, laptop, briefcase, and cell phone, they are claiming turf. They are posturing—making themselves as big as possible—whether or not they realize it. Subliminally, other people at the meeting get that the person holding the most real estate must be the most important.

I have a friend who served for years as a consultant to several large trade associations. Because each of the 30 people sitting around the board table represented a corporate member of "equal importance," the host association arranged chairs in an equidistant manner. When people walked into the room, they started out with comparable territory. As the consultant, however, she always had handouts and other deliverables for the group. Not only did she find the people sitting on either side of her giving up some of their turf for her materials, but she also began commandeering an extra table to hold them. This landgrab exercise of hers became such an integral part of her participation in meetings, that the group began automatically providing extra space for her. As a corollary, they looked forward to seeing the display of deliverables—which ended up in their hands by the end of the meeting. The dual impression was that she had importance (she held a lot of ground), but she was also like Santa Claus (she gave them stuff they wanted).

In a large meeting that you did not call, sit on the same side of the table as the person in charge of the meeting. The best location is next to the person. The proximity accomplishes two things: It associates you with that person's authority, and it makes it far less likely that the person will confront you. And if you're standing, perhaps giving a presentation, and a person at the meeting confronts you, walk toward him. Stand in front of him while you're talking to him. In short, the closer you are to someone in a large setting, the harder it is for him to yell at you. And standing over someone holds tremendous power, especially when you carry a baton, whether figurative (authority) or real (a pointer).

Your objective may not be to reduce conflict, however, but to manage it so you can do a power play. I did this at the initial meeting for *The Guantanamo Guidebook* with people at a TV channel in the UK. When I walked into the room, I saw a horseshoe-shaped table. On one side of the table sat the head of the network, her lawyer, and a production staff of six of their people. Of the gentlemen who sat on the other side, one was their military advisor, and the other I guessed was the psychologist for the project—someone to look out for the good of the volunteers. I sat next to him. I intentionally chose that spot rather than a chair with my team so that words coming out of my mouth would appear to be coming from "us," or really, from him. I opened with, "The first thing I'm concerned about is the welfare of these people. We're going to leave baggage. I want to be sure they're taken care of. It's your lawsuit, but it's my conscience." By doing that, I established a primary concern that they could not attack. The producer then brought up the subject of the using the Koran as an interrogation "weapon." I got stern: "Listen carefully to what I'm going to say. That ain't going to happen. This is an ethical issue. We are not going to throw the Koran around. It has nothing to do with what I believe. It has to do with someone's religion, and not just the bad guys." They pushed back and pushed back, but the message from the "good guys'" side of the table prevailed. I had made myself one of the experts looking out for their good and the good of the volunteers.

Handling Hot Issues

Another type of power play could involve you going into a meeting with the intent of being elected to the head position. Your rivals are also at the meeting. You might even be relatively unknown compared to the competition. One strategy is to use the slightest hint of controversy to establish yourself as a coalition-builder. Wedge yourself in the middle and point out directly how the other candidates are on opposite sides. If you can make them appear to be at odds to the detriment of the group, and then you rise above them.

In contrast, if you're going head to head with an incumbent and you want to win at all costs, first push him into a debate. Next, steer it to a topic that will cause him to behave emotionally. You want him to leak negative emotion—that is, to behave badly. Finally, remind him publicly that the debate is about the issues. It isn't personal. Your objective is to project presidential authority, to convey, in the words of Alexander Haig after President Ronald Reagan was shot: "I am in control here."

A common source of discord at meetings is that people disagree on how to solve a problem. Use control questions, leading questions, and repeat questions to keep the group on track and in cognitive thought. Expect a bad decision to come out of a meeting in which the one who made the most noise won the argument.

In a one-on-one meeting, the touchiest situation would involve some kind of disciplinary action, especially firing. When you fire someone, you can distance yourself from the anxiety by firing the role, not the person. You have to be able to say, "This isn't about you; it's about your performance." An element of planning and preparation helps in this situation. Do monthly counseling with your employees regardless of performance. If someone does well, counsel her in writing. If she does poorly, counsel her in writing. All the good things go on the left and the bad things on the right. When the person gets in serious trouble, hold up that sheet and look at it. Let it guide your judgment.

In a meeting of any size, you have enormous control over how hot issues are handled if you effectively manipulate roles. Your must bring the right person to the dance and you invite the person(s) you want to dance with. You can't necessarily predict what role others will bring into a meeting, but you can work on the premise that any role can only be maintained as long as there is a context for it. Take a great actor portraying King Arthur in *Camelot* and put him in the middle of a play about urban gangs. He won't be able to maintain his character because no one around him treats him as they would King Arthur in

Camelot; no one around him sees him as King Arthur. And if he does manage to continue his portrayal as scripted, it becomes comic because of the incongruity between him and the other actors.

What would the actor have to do to "stay in character?" He would have to leave the script and redefine the role. In a contentious meeting with a CEO, then, you can use trappings, background information, and your own roles and rituals to shift the context just enough to force a role change. You take on the tough decision, you make the problem your problem, and you use body language that signals strength and protection. The result is that you bring out the energetic, relaxed guy who started the company with his own invention. It's the guy who didn't worry about a board of directors or about the PR campaign for a new product.

In personal relationships, people do this all the time. Your husband had a lousy day at work and comes home, still the disgruntled employee, but you "parent" him so he shifts into the role of coddled child. The trick, if there is one, is simply committing wholeheartedly to your role the way a good actor does.

I had a rough meeting with someone at a company where I'd done a lot of consulting. He pushed and got confrontational in a way that struck me as inappropriate. I said, "Look, I know your son and have a lot of respect for him. His name means integrity to me." This man had spent years of his life building that kid into a fine man, so my saying those words pushed aside his tough guy and drew out the father. At that point, I regained control, despite his rank in the company, and we moved forward.

Chapter 12

Direct the Interview

The aim of this chapter is to prevent you from being a victim of an interview or salary negotiation, regardless of which side of the table you're on. You must structure the experience to get the outcome you want.

Get this straight in your mind, first of all: Jobs involve roles; before you go to an interview or conduct one, deliberately assume the appropriate role. You are not the parent, the spouse, the fun date, the tennis player, or the comedian in a job interview. You are selling a solution. If there were no problem, then why would the company advertise for a person to solve it? You need to find the severity of the injury and show why you have value in healing this pain.

Another thing to consider is that you should have expectations of your boss, whether you're near the top or toward the bottom of your company. The set-up is not a one-way street. Establish the fact that you have expectations for your boss early on—right after you're hired. From written goals to regular raises, make it clear what kind of behavior will support you in doing a great job.

Directing a Job Interview

Before you go into the interview, get two things straight in your head. First, you don't have to be the best there is, but you have to be the best there is at the price you're asking. You are the product you're selling, and the product needs to seem as though it's a great value. Second, the likelihood of someone else coming in with an identical skill set is rare, but the perception might be that lots of people have precisely the same skills and talents as you. You have to differentiate yourself from the crowd. Answer this question for yourself: What am I bringing to the table that other people don't have? If candidates with your experience and education are likely to bring A, B, and C, what are your D and E? Your primary differentiator may be that your good friend works for the local paper. Use it. Or, you might be fluent in three languages. Say that, and then explain why that is important. I know that Arabic isn't the most useful language for business in North America, but I wouldn't hesitate to remind a potential employer that a mind that can adapt to new ways of thinking is invaluable.

In the interview, make your moves early in the process to establish a measure of control. That can be a simple as leaning in a little as you shake the person's hand. She backs up to maintain her space—she's already yielding something.

Immediately, you also need to project that you are a person. It's much harder to say "no" to a human being with whom you've forged a connection than with a resumé that happens to have a face and body attached to it. This is one aspect of the value of small talk. The other is that, as you talk about the rainy weather or the fact that you both grew up on a farm, you can baseline the person. Watch for any uncomfortable reaction while you do this, however.

The person may have limited time for the meeting and be signaling you to get to the point. In that case, cut the chat.

Turn this around: You're the one interviewing. You might want to get straight to business so that you can comfortably say "no." Respond to the small talk with a short answer and go directly to your job-related questions.

Look for barriers right away. These can be a table, laptop computer, positioning of arms on a desk—anything that stands between you and the other person. You need to determine up front whether barriers will serve you well in the interview, or undermine you.

As I noted in Chapter 11, the location of your real estate at the table projects a certain message. To whatever extent possible, take advantage of this in a job interview, as well as meetings with your peers. Be early for the interview; hopefully, someone will show you to the room where one or several people at the company will meet with you. The ideal situation is that you will remain in one room as various people move in and out to interview. In that setting, you can angle your chair away from the table to remove the barrier and establish a friendly atmosphere, as if you're welcoming them into your space. In that case, angle another chair as well so that you appear to be partners having a conversation.

Alternatively, you can position yourself on the opposite side of a table if you think a barrier will serve you well—if your leg shakes when you're nervous, for example. If you're covered from the waist down by a barrier such as a table, you don't broadcast the stress as much.

Another way to use the barrier is if you know that several people will be meeting with you at one time. You can put their chairs relatively close together on the other side of a table and hold down the other end alone, as if this is your office and your desk. The arrangement subliminally gives you a certain authority.

Another scenario is that your interviewer might invite you to sit down a table that he's already "marked" as his. For example, he might have books and magazines on a table that sits between you and him. All that paper does is strengthen the barrier between you, and you want to remove it as much as possible. You have two choices: Find some way to reduce the barrier, or find some way to move yourself from behind it. You might reduce it by showing a lot of interest in one of the pieces, really looking at it, and then moving it to the side. You might eliminate it by simply moving to a different chair that's closer to him, perhaps on the premise that you would like to show the person something.

Establishing rapport builds on the preparation you did beforehand—what you know about the interviewer as well as the company—and uses the information you gain from body language and trappings in the interview. For example, a self-assured, accomplished woman can quickly connect on an emotional level with her potential male boss (or client) if she knows that a woman in his personal life shares those traits. Seeing a photo of the wife in a suit might lead her to say, "I met a lawyer who's name is MacDougal. Any chance that's your wife?" If he says, "No, my wife is a lobbyist for pharmaceutical companies," you have key information. If he says, "No, my wife's only contact with medical professionals is at the country club," then that tells you something quite different. In the first instance, he's at ease with and attracted to (we presume) a successful professional woman.

To reinforce the rapport, use body language that projects appealing traits, characteristics that make you someone who would be a pleasure to work with (honesty, genuine interest, energy, and so on). Mirroring helps to establish a comfort level, but make sure that your mirroring doesn't become mimicry. Smile, but not that flashy, posed smile. Use the natural one that friends see.

And when you're the candidate, you need to stay alert for any facial signs or body movement that indicate stress. This person is interviewing you—why would she have stress? Maybe there's something about you that makes her tense, but she couldn't articulate it if you asked her. Maybe she knows you're all wrong for the job and can't find a polite way to say, "This won't work. You should leave now." If you notice eyes down right, for example, your interviewer has reached an emotional state that will not serve you well unless you know exactly how to relieve her pain.

Your interviewer asks you a question where you're weak. What do you say? You need to derail the conversation immediately to loop around to something you know well. Your job opportunity might be director of regional sales for an enterprise software company. You get a question about how you might sell project management software, but your strong suit is purchasing software. A possible segue might be: "I just read an article about the confusion executives face in deciding what kind of project management and purchasing software to buy. From my experience, I know that you can reduce the pain about purchasing software by telling them...." A corollary approach is representing yourself as the voice of the customer: "I know his pain."

On the other hand, if you're the interviewer and you hear this diversion, you can always go back to your own planning and preparation: What questions were "musts" for you? If the question about project management software scored high on your list, then you simply say, "Very interesting. Now how does that lesson apply to project management software?" As the interviewer, you have an inherent advantage. Use it. You don't have to be crude, but you can always restate your question by framing it in new language: "What I'm look for is someone who will be good at selling our new product to large and mid-sized companies. Here's what I need to know...."

At that point, the skilled interviewee could go one of two routes: self-deprecating and truthful, or deceptive. A self-deprecating admission should be honest, but present your assets up front: "My knowledge of enterprise requirements and the people who make purchasing decisions can't be disputed. I just haven't had much experience with project management software." The liar would go a different route, maybe something such as this: "I've sold ten million dollars worth of software to companies (that's the true part) and that includes a lot of project management software (that's the lie part)." If you're good and know how to move the conversation forward, you may get away with that lie.

A pathetic fact is that people get jobs by effectively telling lies such as this every day—one more reason to study the lessons in this book.

Here are four tips for interviewing for a job:

- ◆ Close the airspace; make yourself a person. If your primary motivation for applying for a particular job is that it's close to home, enhance your presentation of qualifications with an honest admission: "I have small children at home and don't want a long commute to keep me away from them. I know I'm well-suited for this job and would be especially happy to go to work here because it's close to my family."

  In conducting interviews for Trane, I once asked a man who wanted to transfer to a better position, "Why are you at Trane? You're fluent in Mandarin Chinese. As a linguist, you're a romantic and romantics don't do well in the air conditioning business."

His elegant and honest answer was: "I've balanced the romantic side of my personality with the love of my wife and family."

"That's the most honest thing anyone has ever said to me in a job interview," I told him, "and honesty means a lot to me." He got the job.

- Don't undersell yourself; avoid discussing your weaknesses. A human resources director once asked me, "What don't you do well?" I said, "You don't have to worry about that. I know my weaknesses and I'll be sure they don't get in the way of good performance." As you might expect, that drew her fire: "Your should disclose your weaknesses ▮ your co-workers. It makes for a better team." I told her that was Communism. That was Mao Tse Tung's tactic in convincing people they should admit what they did wrong.

- Don't just sit there and answer questions. Take over by asking a few of your own: "What are your challenges as a company? What kind of problems are you having that you expect the person in this job to address?" You want to leave with the interviewer thinking that he can't live without you. You understand the problems and want to fix them. You set yourself apart from other people who come in and wonder what the company can do for them. Think of it as a date. If I do nothing but tell you how fantastic I am, how interested will you be in a second date?

- Don't try to be funny. A sense of humor is a very personal trait; what makes you laugh could easily offend the interviewer. Instead of breaking tension and warming up your "audience," you run a high risk of freezing the conversation.

Interviewing After Prolonged Unemployment

People who have been unemployed for a while fill the role of an unemployed person. They adapt to this condition, not necessarily out of choice, but out of circumstance. They begin to adopt the mannerisms, viewpoints, and costumes of an unemployed person. I know because I was there after I first left the Army. I tried to find a good job—and tried and tried—and got jobs that were minimum wage. That was honorable, but I completely disappointed myself. I'd just left the Army with a distinguished record in military interrogation and all I could get was a job that required no thinking. I finally understood what it was like to have my self-esteem eroded to the point that it changed me. That's exactly what I had done to prisoners I interrogated. I accelerated their slide into self-loathing.

The process of going down is very simple. For an unemployed person, the role of "worker" is not being fed so it starts to atrophy. The longer you remain unemployed, the weaker that role of "worker" becomes. It's the same thing that happens to a prisoner of war who had the role of soldier. Without any input to reinforce it, the role wastes away. That takes value out of the whole person at the same time because that role represented something important.

When you work, part of your identity comes from work and the people you experience on a regular basis. You lose the input you get from the "hive," and you lose a certain kind of intelligence, when you work in isolation or find yourself disconnected from a group because you're unemployed.

Being unemployed may also isolate you from friends because they have different schedules and more disposable income. Your life changes. You may lose confidence in your social self because you aren't with people on a daily basis. Essentially, you become a different person—as if you're in captivity. When self-pity and helplessness rise to a level of prominence, then you become a prisoner. The world goes black and white, and every issue is personal. Your spouse says, "Money is getting a little tight." You hear, "You loser! It's your fault we don't have more money."

When you go to your next interview, you will need approval at all costs. You will meet with an authority figure who holds promise of your release from captivity, and you will do anything to make her happy. This is why the interview quickly takes a downward turn. You will answer questions the way she wants them answered, even if that means you don't answer honestly, because you need approval. Any interviewer who hears that thinks, "This sounds like the job description to me." You don't project the role of "worker."

To get out of this desperation, you need to build a firewall between that unemployed person and the rest of you. You'll have the means to do that if you develop a new role tied to accomplishment while you're not working. When I was unemployed for a time, I ran a lot. On a daily basis, I accomplished something new in terms of time, distance, pacing, and other performance measures. Learn something. Build something. Invest quality time with your children. Volunteer at your church. Landscape your mother's yard.

Andy Andrews spent four years in a federal penitentiary because of drug trafficking in the early 1970s. Unlike a lot of other people there for the same thing, Andy let the warden know he could fix cars and trucks. He let him know he had woodworking skills. He let him know he had experience landscaping. Throughout his time in prison, that warden kept him busy, so that when Andy got out, he actually had built a resumé with legitimate accomplishments. Bill Sanchez did the same kind of thing when he was a prisoner of war throughout most of World War II. In both cases, when they left captivity, they were mentally prepared to enter the workforce.

Here are three tips for overcoming the effects of a prolonged unemployment:

- Keep a journal while you're unemployed. Your grasp of the changes that occur while you don't have a job will help you counter the ill effects.

- Whenever you go into an interview, have a recent success in your head. It could be something as simple as having run 10 miles for the first time. Success gives you power.

- Take the focus off the resumé for the first few minutes. Make it clear up front who you are. Describe your unique set of skills and how they match up with the problems that the person in this job is supposed to solve.

Controlling Salary Negotiation

Negotiation of any kind is about limiting options. Hostage negotiators achieve their goal by closing off options for hostage-takers. The hostage-taker locks himself in a building with his captives. The negotiator turns off the power and the phone. A little while later the negotiator provides him with a phone, or turns it back on so they can talk. They begin to talk and the negotiator puts the phone down for a minute, as if something else has come up. By doing this, the negotiator starts to create an expectation of control. She then starts to limit the hostage-taker's options. At some point, the hostage-taker feels his options closing off, which causes a sense of hopelessness. Then, by offering just enough hope, the negotiator woos him out.

To some degree, people gain control over us all the time by limiting our options. You go into a restaurant and order an omelet and raisin toast. Unfortunately, there's no raisin, whole wheat, or white bread today. How's an English muffin?

If you combine a strategy to limit options with your knowledge of stress indicators, you have the upper hand in a salary negotiation.

Trane had hired me to conduct interviews with a number of candidates. Part of my responsibility was to negotiate salaries. One applicant sticks out in my mind because he had a spectrum of desirable qualities—academic, professional, personal—but he managed to short-sell himself because of a few small errors. This highly qualified man did three things wrong:

1. He telegraphed what was important to him—namely, not having to relocate and staying at home as much as possible with his son. With that, he gave me a bargaining chip.

2. He presented his "must have" salary as between $60,000 and $70,000. By implying that he would work for $60,000, he shut out any chance my recommending $70,000.

3. He came into the negotiation knowing very little about me.

Combine these three failures, and he gave me abundant opportunities to limit his options. But he had created none to limit mine. I also knew the techniques of baselining, and he didn't have a clue.

Ideally, by the time you get to salary negotiations, you've done two things: baselined the person with whom you're negotiating, and established your value in the context of that environment. If you're the one asking for a particular salary or fee, you need to know what his face and body do when he's calculating, creating, and having an emotional reaction. When I said that the man I interviewed telegraphed what was important to him, I meant that a reference to his son caused visible emotion. It took very little questioning for me to conclude that the advantages of telecommuting had greater appeal to him than a salary at the upper end of his scale. The lesson here is that telegraphing your personal priorities, sore spots, and concerns can undermine your verbal negotiations. You give the other person prime ways of limiting your options.

A second lesson to draw from his failure is that, if you're the one asking, you should not be the one to throw out the number. Generally, the person who throws out the number first has the lower hand. You need to push the person hiring to give you a framework. This is true of just about any kind of negotiation, not just salary. You want him to establish the limit and, if it's not reasonable to you, then you proceed to the next phase of negotiation.

A third lesson is that he did not project his value to me. He did not effectively communicate, through words or body language, what value he brought to the table in my eyes.

There's also a fourth, hidden lesson here related to planning and preparation. Neither one of us had a great deal of control over the numbers. He did not come in with the leverage to dictate a salary amount. At the same time, I had a narrow window to work with and couldn't go beyond a certain figure. He needed to come in to the situation with as much information as possible on how the company matched position to dollars.

Depending on how facile you are with numbers, or how well you've done your preparation, you can also use minimizing in your negotiations. You ask for $52,500 and the number you get back is $52,000. You look at the interviewer and say, "That's a difference of twenty-five cents an hour. We both know I'm worth that additional twenty-five cents an hour." You might even add, "You could get me started on the job right now or spend more than $500 on the next set of interviews."(Quick trick: The standard work year is 2,000 hours. If the amount you're haggling over is $2,000, then the disputed amount per hour is a dollar.) Be careful, though: Use this ploy once with a person. Repeating it turns you from a clever negotiator into an annoying one.

If you're on the other end of the negotiation, of course, you can also minimize to turn it around. To your employee asking for raise, you can say, "You have seniority here, three weeks paid vacation, good benefits. Do you want to risk it all to start over somewhere else?" Or to a candidate, you might say, "Would you really consider giving up this opportunity for twenty-five cents an hour?"

Fundraisers and pitch artists on infomercials minimize in an analogous way when they remind you that a $120 pledge means nothing more than $10 a month to support your public radio station, or ask, "Isn't clear skin worth $5 a week?"

You do have to monitor reactions as you play these games. If you throw out a firm figure of $72,000 as your base salary requirement, you might see surprise. So, you're probably way too high. If you're close, you can imagine what might happen: His eyes might go hard left to remember what the range of numbers is. And then, his eyes go up right to indicate he's creating how he can move those numbers. After that, he may go to down left, because he's calculating what kind of shift he can afford. And even if you're close, but he really can't afford you at that level, you won't see his eyes move. The alternative is that he knows how to bluff and you're negotiating with a good poker player. Of course, if you see pale skin and thin lips—signs of deception and/ or stress—you might want to call his bluff.

Finally, you may find yourself negotiating a salary or contract terms with someone who hates to talk about money. The very thought of having a financial conversation raises his stress level, so he doesn't go into the process completely logical. Your task then is to make the subject non-emotional. By engaging the person in an open discussion of your worth, and driving toward specifics about what funds are available to pay you for your high performance, you can draw the person out. The approach of "it's only twenty-five cents more an hour" can put the negotiation in the realm of an intellectual exercise that averts an emotional response. Your aim is to make sure the expenditure doesn't "hurt." Subtly reminding the person that it isn't her money—it's company money—can help, too.

A final element to consider in interviews and negotiations is how well you can tip the balance with your presence. With some exceptions, authority comes from people around you giving you authority because of the way you walk and talk. You've undoubtedly encountered people "in charge"—in your office, your platoon, or even your home—that you blow off because they hold rank, but not authority. Take your authority with you into a negotiation.

And watch out that you don't let cultural conditioning hold you back. If you are conditioned to think that women cannot hold authority, for example, then they won't for you in a job interview, a negotiation, or in day-to-day interaction. If your culture has drilled prejudice into you, then you will assume that people who are on the other side of your bias are nor worthy of more money, not able to make good decisions, or something else ridiculous. And what if you're on the receiving end of that bias? What you accept as limits *are* limits. You won't have authority unless you challenge every ritual that holds you back. Where would Oprah Winfrey be if she hadn't done that? As I said before, your authority comes from within. Take it with you into every interview and negotiation.

Chapter 13

Close
the Deal

You can close a deal if you can create a market for your services. As an interrogator, I "create a market" by offering to fix a problem I caused. To illustrate what I mean, I'll tell you something personal. When I was a kid, I had a dream that a man slashed my throat with a knife. As I was bleeding to death, he said to my father, "I'm a doctor. For $500, I can fix that." He closed the deal with my father.

Cold Calling

When I was on the road with friends who brought their dog with them, we found ourselves in a place without any hotel that would accommodate pets. We couldn't just leave the dog in the car, so I picked him up and walked resolutely past the front desk and up to our room. No one said a thing. The moral of the story: Act as though you're doing the right thing and people rarely question you. Cold calling means getting past the gatekeeper, and that won't happen unless you convince that person that you have every right to be there with that dog in your arms.

A cold call should really only be "cold" from the perspective of the person you're calling on. You need to walk in knowing a lot about your subject, even if he knows nothing about you. You need to have enough information so that you can walk in with an understanding of what problem you will solve for the person, what pain you will relieve. You need to get to the point; a decision-maker will not talk to you all day to figure out what you can do for her.

I'll illustrate the way this plays out by returning to the Samantha scenario—only this time, she has more mature technique and handles the meeting correctly. I'll also break it down in terms of planning and preparation, and the phases of interrogation: establish control, establish rapport, the approach phase, the questioning phase, follow-up, and termination.

Scenario: Steady Steps to Closing the Deal

Samantha learned from a former client that the OK Company faced a major product launch. She had a track record in getting post-launch media coverage and decided to pitch her public relations agency to the president of OK Company.

Planning and Preparation

Her document research provided a comprehensive view of the three-year-old company with one exception: finances. As a privately held company, the disclosures on research and development investments, operating budget, and sales/revenue related to the original product were vague. Her research on the president, however, yielded plenty of insights about what approaches she could use to discuss finances openly with him and close a deal.

She asked her former client who had given her the lead to contact the president and recommend her agency. After that, she made an appointment to see him—but only after finding out from his assistant when he would be in the office for several days in a row, not just returning from a trip or on his way out the door. Directly asking the assistant a key question also gave her hot information: "Is your new product coming out in June as you had announced?" Without hesitation, the assistant answered, "Oh no. We just announced to analysts that it'll be out this fall."

Establishing Control

Samantha arrived for her appointment 12 minutes early—not so early that it seemed as though she was snooping and not cutting it so close that she couldn't snoop. She asked if she could use the ladies room and, when she went in, found what she was looking for: an employee who was primping. She engaged her in casual conversation about the company and the president. The president spent a lot of time out of the office, traveling both for business and pleasure. People in the company liked being around him, except for times such as now when he felt lots of pressure from having to delay the product launch. An "oh, by the way" comment told Samantha that the employee thought she had a better shot at a contract than the jerk who came in before and spilled coffee on the carpet.

The new intelligence confirmed that Samantha did have competition, even if it was weak. It also reinforced what Samantha had already decided about the role she chose to make dominant in the meeting—that of "fellow entrepreneur/senior executive." Other roles that had worked for her in the past included "media savvy publicist" and "nurse." The latter was her way of characterizing the expert in crisis PR who had to bandage wounds to a company's image that ruthless reporters had inflicted.

Rhett Johnson, the president of the company, came out of his office to greet her—a good sign. It suggested he had an hospitable nature, but more than that, it got him away from his desk. She realized that the worst-case scenario was that she would meet him with the barrier of a giant executive desk between them. When he ushered her into the office, she saw a small table with two padded, straight-backed chairs on either side. She stood near the chair facing the door and looked around the office as she commented, "You have wonderful taste in furnishings, Rhett." She then pulled the chair out and sat down at the table.

Addressing him by first name and selecting a location for their meeting away from his desk went a long way to establishing her chosen role of fellow entrepreneur/senior executive—that is, "colleague."

Establishing Rapport

Samantha surveyed the room to familiarize herself with her prospect's trappings. She looked for diplomas and awards—possible signs of wanting to impress people—and saw a framed reprint of an article about him. The room furnishings and reprint told her this was a guy who wanted to project success. She noticed his desk had no paper on it, not even a scrap. "This guy must get things done verbally," she thought. "He delegates, so the paperwork lands on somebody else's desk." This told her that he'd probably expect her to deal with others in the company if she got the contract. Two photos behind him told her something about his intimate connections and interests: his wife, and the Tower of London. Because the photos faced out rather than toward him, she wondered what he wanted the pictures to project about himself. That he has relationships? That he likes travel? She remembered what the woman in the restroom had said about him being gone a lot.

Samantha set about to establish rapport and baseline through conversation. Her first question helped confirm that he had, indeed, set aside an hour for their meeting and that he had no changes to the summary agenda she had e-mailed him. She then remarked as she nodded toward his photo: "The Tower of London must be special to you." Rhett admitted that he'd toured it five times. "Five times" told Samantha that her prospect appreciated something solid and long term, that he enjoyed history. Her inner voice cautioned: Stay away coming off as trendy! She asked, "My favorite part was, oh, what do they call that curved structure where they used to keep the Crown Jewels?" Samantha knew perfectly well the answer was Wakefield Tower. It was a control question. She watched his eyes and listened to the tone and pace of his voice. He put his visual cortex in gear and looked up and to the left a bit as he replied, "Wakefield Tower. That octagonal chamber upstairs is magnificent...." Rhett continued briefly with his recollections of the chamber, which clued Samantha into another aspect of his persona: He paid close attention to details. It occurred to her that there may be aspects of his life in which he takes a big-picture view, but with those he cherished he paid close attention to the fine points. "He probably decorated his own office," she thought. In the back of her mind, she thought her competitor spilling coffee on the carpet that Rhett had personally selected and thought, "Man, that blunder set her back."

The minutes of polite chat behind them, Samantha got to the point while she continued to baseline him. She wanted him to know that, as a fellow business executive, time was money and money was a concern: "Rhett, I know you have a little slide in your project. That must be costing you something. I know what happens in a lot of those cases—your promotional budget will drop. What if I can show you a way that you can get maximum impact on a reasonable PR budget so you can continue to focus primary resources on production?" He seemed quite relaxed as he said, "Yes. Go on."

Samantha had successfully established rapport as a fellow world traveler and, more importantly, as a colleague who understood his priorities.

The Approach Phase

Rhett's assistant suddenly knocked on the door. Could he please come out and resolve an issue regarding blueprints for the office expansion? He seemed a little annoyed. This was clearly not the type of detail he chose to care about. When he stepped out of the office, his assistant closed the door. Samantha got the chance she wanted: She quickly went to Rhett's desk and glanced at the one photo he had facing inward. It was Rhett and a women his age—his wife, she presumed—in full leathers standing beside a Harley Davidson.

Aha! She had been planning a primarily pride-and-ego up approach combined with love of success, but now she saw that emotion would play a key role. The most private statement in his entire office broadcasted, "I want freedom. I want to escape on the open road." As his partner in achieving success with the product launch, thereby quickly improving the bottom line, she could help give him that freedom.

The Questioning Phase

When Rhett returned, Samantha asked him to describe the product the company intended to roll out. She saw him shift in his chair, quickly look to the upper left, and then look to the upper right, and then down right. Based on how he'd responded before, his movement in this instance suggested he was first pulling from memory, and then doing a visual construct. Her preliminary conclusion: OK Company's engineers had to redesign some aspect of the product, and this had probably forced a delay of the launch date and cost money. The down-right glance indicated that Rhett had some emotion about the whole thing. In his mind, could the delay have cost him some of the freedom of travel he wanted so much?

To pursue this presumption, Samantha decided to use a few leading questions: How much peace of mind would it give him if he knew the roll-out would generate a lot of attention in the trade press? How positively would it impact advance sales if the "extra" time before the launch involved good press for the beta version of the product? How much easier would his life be if his sales force could do presentations right after the launch with glowing product reviews in hand? She had chosen her words carefully. "Peace of mind" and "easier" were meant to convey the opportunity for freedom—freedom for him to escape the office and hit road with his bike.

The answer to each question gave her two important pieces of information:

1. His emotional attachment to good publicity vis-a-vis sales.

2. A sense of how valuable, in dollars and cents, a strong media relations campaign was to the company.

Confident that she had moved Rhett to a place of trust and even optimism, Samantha then used direct questions to ascertain his budget for public relations. The down-left glance—a calculation—followed by a look down right told her something unfortunate: He probably doesn't have a budget and he doesn't think he can afford to spend money on my services, at least not now. The body language that reinforced her suspicion was Rhett's foot-tapping. He hadn't done it before a direct question about money; he felt stress.

She needed to back off for a minute so she quickly changed her line of questioning to bring him back to a non-stress state. She repeated the essence of her question about preliminary sales to set the stage for her proposal: "These added few months before launch seem like a great opportunity. How much help would it be to spend relatively little money now for the promise of strong advance sales?"

Following Source Leads

The main piece of information Samantha still needed was a precise sense of what fee to propose for creation of a media relations plan and pre-launch services. Her mental notes reminded her that he threw out some impressive numbers related to the possibility of advance sales. She came back to that by asking him about the advance sales for the previous product. "We sold 800 units before the official release date," he said proudly. She did the math in her head. If 800 units was his benchmark of success, and the per-unit cost was $X, then he would feel good if 600 of the more expensive, next-generation product sold in advance. Based on that, she calculated what she could reasonably charge him to support sales at that level.

She was ready to close.

Termination

"In many ways, the delay serves you well," she began. "By launching in the fall, you can take advantage of advance coverage of products premiering at the trade show in Las Vegas." She threw out a few product names from the previous year's show, as well as numbers, references to good reviews—no exact sales or revenue numbers, but she sure made it sound as though other companies had achieved last year what he needed to achieve this year. "Is this what you want?" she asked.

Hearing a "yes," she made one last appeal to the man who wanted to ride away on his Harley before quoted fees: "Without the kind of support we can give you, this project will lock up your time and energy. A man in your position is too busy to deal with things like publicity. We're here to take the burden off of you, to give you the capability to fly a little freer." She then quoted a tight fee range, fully expecting him to agree to the lower end of the range. He did. As they shook on the deal, she said he would receive details of her proposed work program and a contract by Thursday. She asked him if, at that time, she could take him to lunch so she could begin collecting specifics she needed for the plan. He agreed.

Both Sides of the Auto Deal

In a typical auto transaction, the person assuming the role of the interrogator is the one in the sales role. You want to turn that upside down and put yourself, the customer, in the role of interrogator.

The first time I went to buy a new car, I was 23. My wife and I had enough to make a $300 a month payment and nothing to trade in. We owned a beat-up truck that had barely survived a wreck, so we looked like a couple of hillbillies riding around town. At the time, my wife worked for a guy who owned a Cadillac, which we borrowed to go to the dealership. I wanted to project that we had more money than we did. Sure enough, when we arrived, the salesman ran to help us.

He behaved just as an interrogator: He read our trappings. You show up in overalls and a beat-up truck, and he assumes you're in the market for something cheap. You show up in khakis and a Cadillac, and he assumes you're affluent. He then runs an approach based on that assumption. The emphasis may be on the engine, on the success he assumes you want to project, or on your desire to spend as little money as possible—in other words, love of speed/performance, pride-and-ego up, or the incentive of savings.

You need to establish control before he runs that approach. Begin with planning and preparation. Determine precisely how much you have to spend and match it to a set of requirements—a written set of requirements. Sound basic? Most people walk into a dealership the victim of their own poor planning, which is quickly followed by becoming a victim of someone else's excellent planning. Go in with expectations, just as the sales professional goes in with expectations.

The trappings of your planning and preparation might include printouts from Websites, the Blue Book, and your personal checklist. These props enable you to take over as the person who asks the questions. Take full advantage of the fact that you can go online and find out what the vehicle of your dream costs in 50 states and in every country from Aruba to Zambia.

I'm suggesting two styles of handling an auto negotiation, depending on what you believe gives you greater control with the particular target.

Style #1

Go to him, shake hands, and introduce yourself. When he says, "What are you in the market for, Sue?" you reply, "I'm looking."

"You must have some idea of what you're looking for?"

"I do." And then you begin to walk through the show room toward the pick-up trucks or the sports cars, or the SUVs, depending on what category vehicle you want. By doing this, you are displacing his expectations. He gets a little walk-on-eggshells feeling that puts in you in control. Very likely, he'll try to begin accommodating you by asking how much you have to spend. At this point, the transaction is similar to a salary negotiation: Don't talk numbers up front. Don't tell him what you have to spend; lay out your requirements. Let him show you what cars on the lot meet your description.

Curb your enthusiasm when you look the vehicles, even the ones you like. Keep asking questions that displace his expectations: "Why are these trucks at the back of the lot?" "Can you explain the fuel efficiency numbers on this model? I read they're inflated." Privately refer to the Blue Book and papers in your hands when he answers your questions. Make notes. Check things off your list.

Especially in the case of used cars, find specific things wrong with the inventory. Too many miles. Scratches that look as though the car was wrapped in barbed wire. Ugly paint. Question previous ownership. Your approach is pride-and-ego down, and you invite an incentive approach from him.

I'm not encouraging you abandon all politeness. There is a way to carry off pride-and-ego down that doesn't turn your negotiation into an exercise in humiliation. I am urging you to remain objective, however. Spotting what's wrong with the cars holds you in that state better than focusing on how great the cars are. It will prevent you from surrendering control of the "interrogation."

Walk past the one you think you want. Review the entire line-up. Review your notes. Then ask him: "What are your prices on the blue one, white one, and red one?" or however you want to designate the candidate vehicles. When he says, "Give me a minute," which is a fairly standard ploy to get you to sit there and savor the idea of owning the one you really want, just sit down with your notes and read them.

In response to price, use the information you have in your hands: "Why is yours $2,000 more than the Blue Book value? What can you bring it down to rather than have me buy it from this other dealership?" Or you could simply say, "Too much. I'm willing to pay $18,000. I won't touch it for $23,000."

During this phase, read your source. Do you see any emotion leaking, any signs of stress? When you ask the hard questions of "why" and "what can you do for me," notice whether he's calculating—down left with the eyes, or perhaps a tilt of the head—or down right—a sign that you've triggered some emotion. He may not know the answer to the question and may therefore try to make something up, or he may not want to give you the answer. It could be that bringing down the price any more is possible, but he'd lose so much in commission, the deal wouldn't be worth the time he'd have to invest in closing it.

Style #2

Go to him, shake hands, and introduce yourself. When he says, "What are you in the market for, Sue?" you open with pride-and-ego up: "What a beautiful showroom. I've heard you run a really good business here." Pride-and-ego down: You have also heard that the model you're interested in doesn't hold its value in the secondary market; the Website printouts in your hand substantiate that. Pride-and-ego up: You seem delighted at the way he addressed your issue. Pride-and-ego down: Unfortunately, you add, that you know the manufacturer has been plagued with recall problems, and that the model is notoriously fuel inefficient. Pride-and-ego up: You're delighted to have someone as knowledgeable as he is addressing your concerns.

In the process of pushing him up and pulling him down, you demonstrate genuine knowledge about the car while you displace his expectations. Watch his body language to be sure he addresses your concerns truthfully—that he isn't making up responses on the fly. If he does, you can move forward with the deal. If you suspect deceit, walk away, not matter now much you like car. There are other cars in the universe.

• • •

For all you car salesmen and women out there, now it's your turn. You already know effective approach lines such as, "Someone with your class deserves this car." "After raising three kids, it's about time you drove a car you enjoyed." "You look happy driving that car." Many of you also do one other thing right in terms of playing on your customers' emotions, but you do it by accident. Someone in training probably told you that most people are right-handed, so when you present purchase documents, you typically put the pen on the right side of the person. This is more than a convenience. Your customers have to look down right to grab the pen and sign on the line—you've subconsciously stimulated an emotional connection to the purchase. If they're far enough into the deal to have a pen in front of them, this action probably reinforces a good feeling about buying the vehicle. Trying using this a few steps prior in the process. Use your hot approach lines while pointing to the car in such a way that your customer looks down right at it. Say them while slipping the brochure for that car across the desk so the customer looks down right.

And if you're the customer, move the pen to the left so you can calculate whether or not the deal makes sense.

Lawyers and Juries

The courtroom isn't daily life, even for lawyers, and it's particularly alien to the rest of us. The trappings and rituals alone can induce such stress that baselining presents unique challenges. If you're a lawyer, "closing the deal" rests on good basic questioning and determining the drives and learning styles of potential jurors and witnesses. If you're on the other end of the questions, your job is straightforward: Stay calm and tell the truth.

Jury Selection

Allan R. Stein, professor at the Rutgers University School of Law and co-author of a civil procedure casebook, notes that in jury selection, the rule is "lots of rules." Around the country, a number of elements vary. Who asks the questions? Are they canned questions, mandatory for each set of potential jurors? Can the litigator ask open-ended questions? Will the judge accept questions from the lawyers?

An auditory or visual control question that tells you whether the person is left-memory or right-memory is what you need for baselining. Knowing this alone will provide you with insight into the general bent of a person, even if later questions are "yes" or "no." Cognitive and emotional thought are, in my experience, always in the same locations: Eyes go down right when accessing the emotional portion of the brain and eyes go down left when accessing the cognitive function of the brain.

For open-ended questions, the capability to allow the person to recall visual memory or auditory memory may be key if your case ties closely to visual or auditory elements.

Body Language

On a flight, I shared the row with a trial lawyer. We were returning from Washington, D.C., where I had just taught classes in body language. Knowing this prompted a story of his defense of an alleged rapist. He had presented the case and, as he closed, he noticed a female juror who looked at him and broke down in tears. He felt confident that he had gotten though to her. When the jury unanimously found the man guilty, he asked her about the demonstration. Her response was that, when she looked at him, she couldn't imagine how anyone could defend that son of a bitch who was on trial. He had made a broad assumption based on one moment in time, one small piece of body language. The challenge is to recognize patterns of reactions before you jump to conclusions about a single reaction.

Questioning

Effective questions get the most information in the shortest amount of time possible. This is the stated mission of interrogation, as it is yours in using these tools. Maintaining a lead sheet, whether virtual or real, helps to keep you on track, using the right questions to drive toward the answers you need.

Your questions should be clear and concise and should, in most cases, elicit a narrative response. The primary reason for a narrative response is the ability to corroborate or refute facts earlier or later in questioning. Questions should use basic interrogatives. Questions such as "Explain the situation..." allow freewheeling and let the person's mind decide which data you are given or not given. When questions follow these formats they block options and allow the source responding to spiral into your control pattern. Good questions allow the source to recall information in the way it was stored and allow the questioner to keep track.

Canned Questions

Lawyers are similar to interrogators in their adaptability and mutability of daily work. In the intelligence business, we use a model called the "intelligence support brief" to help better understand the concepts and types of questions to ask. From this, we prepare canned questions for specific issues that are either too detailed or technical to remember. Realizing that you must become a specialist for a day, this may be of tremendous assistance for lawyers as well.

Bad Questions

Have you heard there's no such thing as a bad question? Garbage. Here are some of them in the context of the courtroom:

* Leading questions can be destructive to truth collecting but also cause you to miss real details by overlooking source leads.
* Negative questions create a confusing dilemma for all but the most precise grammarians. ("Why didn't you not go to the library after you finished shopping?)
* Compound questions allow the source to answer either/or. They waste your time and cause confusion. Compound questions also offer a prime opportunity to lead you off the path.
* Vague questions allow the source to redirect your conversation.

Leads

Leads are simply the hooks in conversation or the responses that key the mind to a new topic. Think of the twists and turns that daily conversations take. If you cannot set priorities on leads, the result is the squirrel in the highway. Leads fall into three types:

1. Hot: They are more important than your current line of questions and should be exploited now.
2. Cold: They are good to know but should wait until the current line of questioning is complete.
3. Misleads/Disinformation: Your source has intentionally planted juicy-sounding tidbits that sound as if they're hot leads to get off track.

Transitioning from an exploited hot lead requires practice. Without taking notes to remember where you left the path, the likelihood of returning to it is low. I have used note-takers to keep informed of where I left the path. I've also manipulated the conversation to a keyword that I knew would resurface as I finished exploiting the lead.

Just as interrogators do, lawyers in a courtroom generally work within time constraints toward a goal. Using the tools, personality types, baselining, applying stress, approaches, and good questioning to exploit information will make your time more productive.

Ultimately, the real challenge is to tie the juror's perception of success to your success. You have to limit the outcomes to what is good for you and the juror, or what is failure for the juror if your success isn't considered.

In the Susan Smith trial in South Carolina, the jury quickly found her guilty of murder. In the sentencing phase, this woman convicted of murdering her two children was sentenced to life in prison instead of death in the electric chair. Jurors later said their decision was based in part on the closeness of the community and the impact of the pain Susan's family had suffered as part of the trial. This is a prime example of tying the success of the argument to the well being of the jury. It is a binary decision that will only allow success for the juror if Susan wins as well.

Section V:

Self-Defense

Chapter 14

How to Avoid Falling for These Techniques

Identifying the Problem

You may have jumped to this chapter because you suspect that someone is using these techniques on you—not in a good way. Let me assure you: You don't have to know how to use the techniques to be able to recognize that you're a victim of them. You notice the approaches; you don't have to have names for them. You feel scrutinized. First, ask yourself why that person might be doing it. Second, consider that, if someone has gone to all that effort to extract information from you or force a change, maybe you should get out of that relationship now. The straightforward path to self-defense could be divorce or a new job.

The simplest self-defense advice I can give you is to say, "Don't toy with me" when you become certain that another person is trying to manipulate you with these techniques. A slightly more complex defense is to be cognizant of where your own eyes go and of what emotions your body is starting to leak. Skimming the rest of this book will give you clues as to how you must be self-aware.

The rest of this chapter gets a lot more complicated in exploring your options on self-defense, both proactive and reactive.

You'll know for certain that someone is using these techniques on you if you feel that you're a bad rider on a good horse. I've watched an inexperienced rider mount a horse whose job in life is to carry riders. He'll use reins and kicks in an effort to get the horse to behave. With no ceremony or display of emotion, the horse will saunter over to a fence and rub the rider's leg on it so hard that he begs for mercy. If that's how you feel, you need to know how to get that person to back away from the fence.

Hostage Survival in Business

In a meeting where your employer or a colleague denigrates your performance or judgment, you need to adopt the survival mechanism of a hostage. The situation could be a one-on-one with your boss who wants to fire you, or it could be a large meeting in which someone wants you to lose ground. Your role as an employee of a company is a living role that gets constant feedback from your employer. It isn't the whole "you"—it's one of your roles—and that role is being battered in the meeting. That attack is life-threatening in terms of your role. You have to do only one thing well: survive. The steps to doing that are:

- ◆ Make yourself a person. The individual attacking you has to see you fully human. In Ashley Smith's encounter in March 2005 with killer Brian Nichols, she asked him questions and told him personal facts that engendered a bond with him. As he came to know her more as a living being, his ability to harm her diminished. If your boss calls you in to fire you, you have to make sure he knows you're a person, not an object, and why that person is an integral part of his daily business. You have to bond with him to make sure he sees you as an ally, so that looking out for your interests means looking out for his own. Someone—maybe him—specially chose you for this job. Firing you then seems more as a failure on his part than a dispassionate, necessary action. (Note how this is a twist on the advice in Chapter 13 on firing: If you're on the other end, you focus on the role, not the whole person. In neither case is the employee an object, however.)

* Do what you do best. I may bring forth the part of me that's confident, powerful, and knowledgeable. Ashley Smith brought forth the part of her that's caring, spiritual, and trustworthy. You may want to bring forth the nerd who knows how to fix problems that no one else can fix, or the nice guy who builds morale when other employees are in a funk.

Hostage Survival in Love

The best self-defense in an argument of love, as well as in business, is to personalize the argument—to make it dangerous for the person to continue that line of thought because his attack on you is an attack on himself. You want the person to have a vested interest in keeping you whole. Fundamentally, it's a variation of the argument you use with the boss trying to fire you: "You chose me and you're a smart person, so how bad could I be?"

Unfortunately, in arguments at home, I know it's not as simple as that. Maybe the best you can hope for is that you can escape the argument with some self-respect intact. While someone is attacking you verbally, look for his weaknesses. Don't even rebut right away—or at all. Just store up the factual errors, the missteps in logic, the emotional responses. Let those bonehead mistakes build you up the whole time that person is trying to tear you down.

Do not allow circular logic. Circular logic is nothing more than using a step from your thought process as a founding principle for the process. Consider the following example:

> "That is the hardest mountain around here to climb."
>
> "I climbed that mountain, so I'm in shape."
>
> "I'm in shape, so I can climb mountains."
>
> "I climbed that mountain and it took a lot out of me, but I'm in shape so that must be the hardest mountain around here to climb."

We live in a time when our lives are so saturated with media that we can have a hard time separating fact from fiction. Visit *www.urbanlegends.com* if you want a sampling of the ridiculous things that people believe—many things built on circular logic. Any time you are dealing with someone who cannot define a reason for something, challenge where it came from. Much of the time, you will find the argument relies on the original supposition to support its existence. Circular logic in arguments allows someone to take you down a twisted path with no foundation in facts. When someone projects his failures on you because you hired him and firing him would reflect on you, that is circular logic. Defend against it with real logic.

When I was a 21-year-old Specialist (E4), I had a Sergeant Major yell at me for 45 minutes. As part of his rant, he threw some expletives at me and barked, "You'll never wear green tabs in my battalion." Green tabs are a designation that infantry and combat arms troops wear when they achieve a leadership post. I didn't have a Military Occupation Specialty, or MOS, that would have qualified me to earn green tabs. After 35 years in the Army, this guy should have known that. His ignorance amused me, which distanced me from his tirade. This is exactly the kind of stupidity you want to focus on when someone rages at you.

Another part of your self-defense strategy is telegraphing to the person what he is allowed to attack you on. For example, I want you to attack the red-headed kid with big ears. I know how to defend against that. I don't want you to attack my being incompetent in fixing the roof, or my procrastination in fixing the roof that now leaks. If I'm guilty of those things, my defenses are lower.

What is your spouse likely to pick on you for? You're fat. You're skinny. You have a big nose. You walk into walls. You drive into walls. You flunked 10th grade. You're a lousy cook. You're unemployed. You can't spell. You drink too much. Whatever it is, you already know it about yourself. Put a key word in your head that puts you in a strong defensive mode and make it ring out over and over again when someone mentions it in an attack on you. You have to be able to think: If that's all you got, then you're inept. There's a lot more to me than that, and you can't touch it.

To reiterate, three techniques that will help you leave the argument with some measure of self-respect and mental clarity are:

- Neutralize the effect of the verbal attack by focusing on the flaws in it.
- Project the part of you that person is allowed to attack. Focus attention on an aspect of you that you know how to defend. You want to avoid inviting any words or actions that will put you in limbic mode.
- Activate your force field. You live with this person. You know what the basis for his or her attacks are. Have protective thoughts

firmly planted in your head, "If I hear X, I think of Y."

And when you find yourself slipping into limbic mode, get yourself out of it immediately. Visualize. Figure out how much it would cost to take a weeklong vacation in Cancun. Take any other action that will pull you back into cognitive thought.

Anticipating Approaches

Approaches you are likely to use in business are the same ones you want to have used on you. By that I mean, your best defense against someone using flattery, emotion, or subtle bribery to get information or a desired action out of you is for you to invite an approach for which you are prepared. You decide who comes to the dance and it won't be the person in you who is vulnerable to that approach.

For example, you can invite a pride-and-ego down approach by telegraphing that you're self-conscious about something. You have gray hair coming in, so you color it or wear a hat to disguise that sign of aging that "makes you uncomfortable." So, that's what he tries to use as leverage. Great—you have no problem with aging and no matter what he says, you're resistant to that kind of approach. He can go on and on about "you old hag" and he will not increase his leverage on you.

The advantage to you in this kind of abusive situation is that you can remain in control of your emotions. You have the distance you need to really listen to what he's trying to push you to do instead of react to an insult.

In a business situation, an easy way to invite an approach is to put particular pictures on the wall of your office. Put up your degrees, awards, and a picture of you with the President of the United States and you will surely hear pride-and-ego up approaches. Pictures of your wife and family invite an emotional approach. You want to talk about your family—it's easy—and the photos invite that conversation. Talking about your family gives the person no edge with you. At the same time you get to baseline the other person to run your own approach. If you want someone to use an incentive approach, suggest what means a lot to you: fame, money, freedom, 356-bit encryption, and so forth.

In the last chapter, I gave you a victorious Samantha who closed the deal because she had a lock on her prospect's body language, trappings, information sorting style, and so on. What if that prospect knew just as much as she did and set her up? What if they had read the same book!

Scenario: Closing the Deal From the Prospect's Point of View

Rhett had come out of his office to greet Samantha so he could see what she was doing as she waited. Whenever he saw people who had come to solicit his business just staring at the wall and drinking coffee, he wondered if they would waste his time, too.

Rhett always held small meetings such as this one at the table Samantha chose because it sat in the open. Any nervous twitch or fumbling with paper would be obvious. He admired her confidence for proceeding straight to it. He put the Tower of London photo up purely as bait. No question about it, he loved travel and, in fact, had been to the Tower five times, but he displayed the picture solely to see how observant his guests were. At the very least a "what's that?" told him the person had enough sense to know that a photo that was so prominently positioned must have importance to him.

When Samantha got right to the point of her visit, Rhett saw that she leaked a little emotion. Her index finger rubbed over her thumb—a tiny auto-erotic gesture that helped her adapt. "Good," he thought. She's not arrogant and she's not taking it for granted that I'll respond to her directness. He concluded that, so far, he liked her style and that, yes, she had done a good job of establishing rapport with him.

He had to admit that her approach had appeal. It also occurred to him that her leading questions didn't come from nowhere. He never did figure out that she had seen the photo of him and his Harley; he concluded that something about him projected, "I don't want to spend my days and nights worried about this company. I want other people to do their jobs so my life has balance."

As Samantha asked some of the tough questions that led to a discussion of money, he noticed again that her right index finger rubbed over thumb. Now, she seemed to know it, though, and she picked up the pen she had used for note-taking and simply held it, as if she were channeling excess energy into it.

He decided he needed to see how well she handled pressure—she'd have to deal with a lot of during the product launch—so he pushed her to what he thought would be a very uncomfortable position. "The more I think about our slip in this product release, the more I realize that PR isn't my priority right now. I appreciate your coming in, but this conversation is probably premature. I won't get my head back on this part of the problem for a month or two." Rhett paused and watched her. Eyes down left. She was calculating, not responding emotionally. No finger rubbing either. She sat up straight in the chair and leaned it, as if to say, "I'm ready for this." So he continued, "We don't have any news to put out right now, so I figure we won't need your services until we do."

Samantha's planning and preparation served her well. She knew he might go in this direction—any smart negotiator would—and she was ready: "I understand that, Rhett." By using his name, she made the statement personal. "But in my business, just like yours, I know that preparation is everything. Before news breaks, you have to have your positioning statements, your campaign objectives, and every other aspect of the plan. Your news has to hit the right people with the right words and the right time. You want your announcement to be one in a million, not one *of* a million." She could not have played that better, he thought.

By the time he gave her figures on the unit sales of the first product, he had already decided to hire her. What he didn't reveal was the fact that the margin on the new product was 5 percent better than the margin on the first one. If her work did generate advance sales of 600 units, he'd see a magnificent profit—higher than she could have calculated.

His "candor" on sales of the first product had invited an incentive approach and she went for it. He gladly accepted the low-end figure in her bid range and concluded, "She'll make plenty out of this deal. And doing business with me will make her deal-making skills sharper."

Fending Off Approaches

The approaches that you're likely to encounter in love and business have straightforward defenses. I've suggested a few here, and you will likely come up with others. The one thing all defenses have in common, however, is the need to remain or get back into cognitive thought.

- ◆ Direct. Don't answer the question. Condition the question to take the conversation in a different direction.

- Incentive. Nothing comes without a price in business. If someone offers to placate your needs by going to extraordinary measures, look for the hidden price tag. Don't immediately make a decision based on what appears to be an incentive approach. Put distance, in terms of time and space, between you and the person before you respond to the offer. In a relationship, it's a different story: There are no-strings gifts of love. An offer such as that is not an approach, though. The incentive approach in a relationship means that your spouse or partner wants a concession or action from you and is willing to bribe you for it with sex or dinner or an offer to take the kids off your hands for a day. The same guidance applies here as it does in business: Don't respond immediately. Distance from the person and the offer will improve your perspective.

- Emotion. Don't let someone in a business meeting know what you love or hate. In a relationship, this isn't an option, so your best defense is cognitive thought. When you feel someone pushing you toward an outcome you don't want by using love of kids or home or hatred of your mother-in-law, you must use one of the techniques I've suggested to engage your primate brain.

- Fear-up. Although you hopefully never see fear-up harsh in any circumstance, you are likely to experience fear-up mild. People fall for fear up because they have something to hide. Your best defense against it is to get the issue out in the open. It's important to distinguish between merely berating someone and using fear up as an approach to get information or drive to an outcome. The example I used in Chapter 5 of Ann, the civilian being interrogated for a security clearance, illustrates a fear-up (mild) approach related to her partying.

* Futility. The futility approach in love and business is ridiculous. Just don't fall for it. You always have options.

Sidetracking

A common way of tracking down leads that seem insignificant but garner huge returns is through conversation that trails on and on, seemingly going nowhere. Every once in a while, the interrogator will ask a question, which may or may not signal real interest. Some people have learned how to do this to extract important business information at cocktail parties. Some people have learned this tactic works on someone they want to take home from a bar. You've no doubt encountered this on some level and thought later, "I can't believe I told her that!" The real trick here is to take control of the conversation and lead the conversation to a fruitless end. Everyone knows someone who does this naturally. I once worked with an interrogator who, by her very nature, would bring every conversation back to horses. It maddened most folks, but I could tolerate it. I could turn the conversation as well because I knew enough about horses to ask questions she couldn't comfortably answer.

If you know someone is collecting information, transfer the subject to one without a return path. Focus on a concept or word that will take your conversation so off track that you can't get back. You'll accomplish your goal of evasion without seeming impolite. For example,

the representative of another company you meet at conference reception talks about all the traveling she's been
doing lately. Her objective is to find out if you've been
traveling a lot, too, because where you've been might clue
her in to the new markets your company wants to pen-
etrate. You give a broad smile and say, "I've finally found
a way I love to travel. My wife and I hop on my Harley and
take off down the highway. Makes your own neighborhood seem exotic! Have you ever done a trip on a motor-
cycle?" At that point, dragging you back to a conversation
about business is not only difficult, but it probably con-
firms your suspicion about her motives for bringing up
the subject.

Look at the challenge from another angle: You're the
one lying. You wake up to the fact that someone is questioning you because she doesn't believe your story. You
hear questions related to time of occurrence, nature of an
event, sequence of action, or other request for a level of
detail that seems to spotlight an inordinate curiosity.
Whether you're lying or not, you can use the question to
take the inquisitive skeptic down a path of your choosing.

You've just lied by omission about your early morning run. You say that you set a personal record by doing
7½-minute miles and that you ran eight miles. In truth,
you did a couple of 7½-minute miles surrounded by six
10-minute miles. The person asks you when you left the
house; she was thinking of calling you this morning, but
wasn't sure what time you usually get up. You respond
that you got up at 6:30 and were out the door by 6:45. At
some point later, she finds a casual way of asking when
you returned from your run. Your response to sidetrack
her away from scrutiny of your lie might be, "I know
exactly when I got back because I have a function on my
watch that helps me time my runs. In fact, it even has a
heart monitor. Have you ever seen one of these things?

It's amazing. Let me show it to you." And you've slyly managed to avoid the truth—at least for the moment.

I don't recommend that you practice this. Pointless and seemingly harmless lies such as this can haunt you more than you may realize.

You could also be on the receiving end of a sidetrack. Without even giving it thought, people commonly undermine the control a boss or partner is trying to establish by verbally squirming or shuffling. You call an employee in to discuss a performance problem and he looks at his watch to say that he only has five minutes because he's trying to fix a problem that you told him to fix. You tell your spouse you want to talk about the family budget and he starts thanking you for the amazing birthday dinner you made him. Articulating the specific reasons for the meeting will center the conversation and help you regain control. Think about it: Why are you talking to this person at this time about this topic?

Evasion

Conditioning a question is an evasive maneuver designed to conceal the facts. It allows you to respond with truth that is, something that's true to you—but it doesn't tell the questioner what he wants to know.

When President Clinton said, "I did not have sexual relations with that woman" in response to a question about Monica Lewinsky, he conditioned the question. And from the legal analyses to the jokes, this comment sparked conversations about truth-telling because people knew that the questioner aimed for a "yes" or "no" answer. Instead, President Clinton responded with a statement that was true to him. Recently, in taping a British television show on interrogation techniques, I began my questioning of one of the volunteer "prisoners" with, "What were you doing there?" He responded, "I wasn't doing anything wrong." He could look me straight in the eye and tell the truth with that statement, but he obviously wasn't answering *my* question.

How many times have you done this over embarrassing matters? Your wife says, "Honey, the car has an awful scratch on the passenger's side. Did you hit something?" Your answer: "I did not run into anything with the car!"

The truth: You let go of a heavily loaded shopping cart at Wal-Mart and it scraped the side of the car. By the way, this man's wife would know he was masking the truth if he usually uses contractions, but did not in making this assertion. Such deviations from speech patterns highlight deception.

Conditioning the question, or framing a question, is one technique used to perpetrate dishonesty without (technically speaking) lying. So how do you get past that clever language game, often played in courtrooms, to know that the subject is deceiving you on some level? You give auditory signals—pitch, tone of voice, and choice of words—when you are lying that combine with shifts if your body posture, facial micro-gestures and the other indicators I've described earlier.

Exercise

Listen to ambassadors, legislators, and other officials on the news. How often do they answer a "yes" or "no" question directly? How often do they condition the question and provide a rehearsed answer?

Defusing

To defuse a potentially confrontational situation, particularly one in which someone is trying to nail you in front of others, you should rely on your talents and background. Here's a time to be funny, highbrow, folksy, or whatever else comes naturally to shift the emotional states of people around you or even derail someone in a line of questioning.

Within the United States, how certain terms are used telegraphs where a person is from. A native Georgian will likely use "Coke" as a generic term for "soda," which is the same as "soft drink" in Pennsylvania. A simple regionalism such as this puts people at ease by reminding them of a common bond. A regional expression can also take the heat off you if it's something the group isn't likely to have heard before. In a conference call with people from various parts of the country, I once put a confrontational group back on track by saying, "You've got to state your case clearly. I'm like a hog with a wrist watch when it comes to finance." Except for the Texan on the phone, no one had heard that before, so they laughed and became a lot more accommodating.

Now turn the situation around: Pay attention to these types of quips if you are on the offensive. Folksy expressions can be so funny and endearing that they not only take you off point, but they humanize the person to a degree that makes it difficult for you to engage him. Southern men—and I can say this because I am one—are masterful at making self-deprecating comments. If we want you to think we are less intelligent or powerful or wealthy than we are, we know how to do it by using homespun phrases.

Traditionally, Southerners also do not get confrontational with the same alacrity as someone from the Northeast. If you are from the South and an associate from New Jersey gets in your face, use whatever tools you can to stay in cognitive thought. That outburst, that language—it means nothing, y'all. And if you're from the Northeast, you know that this behavior will likely put someone from the South in limbic mode pretty quickly. You can accelerate your process just by doing what comes naturally to you, but it appears to be a fear-up approach to the person you're addressing.

Creating Memory

I was born with the tools for deception. I have the type of mind that allows me to imagine the possibilities to the point of reality. If you fit in the intuiting/feeling temperament type, you may have this "gift," too. Test yourself: Try to commit to memory the vision of a simple deceit—say, changing a flat tire on your car this morning. Can you get yourself to the point where you access it on your visual memory side?

Even my mind, with its unique qualifications to lie, can be tricked under high pressure. Very aware of that fact when I was a student at SERE school, I took a photo of my ex-wife, a photo of my nephew, and my wedding ring. My interrogators seized on the photo of my wife, a blond, and my nephew (supposed son), who is brunette. "How could a blond and a redhead produce a little boy with brown hair?" they yelled as they called my wife all sorts of derogatory names. I was able to tell them which hospital he was born in, how old he was, his birthday, his middle name, and a plethora of other details. This was simple transference of facts from my brother's life to support the details. For those who cannot visualize lies as facts, transference is your best recourse. Realize this is not going to protect you in high limbic thought and that your chances against a good interrogator are low. But in daily life, unless you are in a darker line of work, this should work for you.

Confronting

I opened this chapter by recommending "don't toy with me" as a legitimate comeback to a manipulator. Sometimes confrontation has to be less obvious.

Body language holds tremendous power in both establishing control and self-defense. We all know from social and business interactions that stature can change the way you relate to someone and either establish control or disrupt someone's control. Regardless of your size, weight, or chest measurement, you can use what you have to make your point: Don't mess with me. Sit up straight, lean forward, square your shoulders, and baton with your arm, and you can convey power regardless of your size. Watch short politicians for clues on how to do this. In *The Great Dictator*, Charlie Chaplin's Hitler character, Adenoid Hynkel, plays on the importance of stature in a scene when the relatively short dictator meets the Mussolini character, who is tall. Failing to keep his rival for world domination vertically challenged with chairs of different heights, Chaplin finally resorts to standing on his desk to dramatize his superiority. I don't recommend you do this because I've actually seen a variation of this done in an Asian country and, believe me, it's still funny.

A person with certain physical attributes—looks, height, girth, and even a disability—can get away with establishing an advantage only when he is in an encounter with someone who lacks confidence, or facts, or brains, or a plan.

The first thing to keep in mind is that, any time a person relies primarily on any of these externals as leverage to get what he wants, he is vulnerable. You can take away that person's power related to physical characteristics very easily with your confidence, facts, and brains, and/or a plan. What's in your head is the most powerful tool you have, and it's not a matter of IQ. It's your ability to think under stress, your ability to adapt your ability to stress, and to project your outcome.

The intended impact of displaying physical dominance is that you feel subservient: Don't let it have the intended impact. If you suspect someone is running this game on you, ask yourself how you feel. They can establish control of the meeting—sometimes that's appropriate—but that doesn't mean they control you.

Quick Stress-Release Tips

Mechanisms for quick stress-release can help you regain control and move back into cognitive thought when someone is hammering you. Try one or all of these to see what calms you down quickly:

- Breathe deeply through your nose.
- Yawn.
- Make a horse sound with your mouth. As your cheeks flap loosely, you relax the facial muscles, which affect the level of tension in your entire body. This one's a bit obvious, but if you want to interrupt the person's train of thought while you regain your composure, this works great.
- Sneeze. In humans, a sneeze can be a photo-sympathetic response—that is, a response to light. A horse's response is head-shaking, and I actually discovered the fact about the sneeze from watching my horses and wondering what the human counterpart was. Practice inducing a sneeze in the sunlight or with a bright light in the face. Just don't look directly at the sun or the bulb. If you pluck your eyebrows, you've probably had a similar sensation and either

sneezed or felt as though you were going to sneeze.

If All Else Fails

You can have all the tools you need to maneuver people toward your desired outcome and still not achieve it. Why?

1. You lack the self-respect and/or self-confidence to use them.
2. You have met someone with a hard core—someone who is self-aware and confident of who he is—and who has tools to match yours.

If you fall into the first category, I can't change you, but I can offer advice that you can definitely follow: Do your planning and preparation. That is, research your source, pay attention to facial signs and body language, note rituals and trappings, think about what approach would be the best for the circumstances, and think of the questions you want answered. Even if you never execute the next set of moves, you have prepared yourself to spot a liar.

As for the second category, have fun with him or her. The likely outcome of that encounter is that you both tell the truth. How bad is that?

Conclusion

One of the reasons why you should not use these techniques casually with someone you're involved with is that the feeling of manipulation can make people feel bubbly. You didn't expect to see that, did you? In reality, your expertise in exploiting a person's feelings and driving him or her to an outcome of your design can enhance your appeal. In a way, you become more attractive, at least while you're around. The downside is that, when you leave, you can leave an aftertaste. The person starts to realize that being in your presence feels good but wonders why doubts creep in when you're gone. That perception can have a chilling effect on a relationship.

Salespeople who effectively manipulate their customers' behavior—whether consciously using these techniques or just doing "what comes naturally"—face a similar problem: They have to stay in constant contact to make sure the customer feels good. Of course, if the manipulator works at a storefront electronics store or for a telemarketing firm, why would she care about the customer feeling good? She probably wouldn't. But as a customer, you're likely to associate an icky feeling with the product you bought and/or the company.

An unintended consequence of this book is that you may, at least initially, feel quite transparent and mortal.

As you start to understand how easy it is to read people and understand your drives, you may become self-conscious of your every movement. Relax. And practice. That way, you stay a step ahead.

Glossary

Batoning. Using a body part, often an arm, to drive home a point; called batoning because the person uses the body part as a conductor uses a baton.

Circadian rhythm. "The rhythmic repetition of certain phenomena in living organisms at about the same time each day," according to the Joint Commission on the Accreditation of Health Care Organizations glossary (*www.jcaho.org*). Interrogators manipulate circadian rhythm with light, temperature, and food to disorient a source, particularly when trying to extract time-sensitive information.

Circular logic. Going back to a presumption to make a comment, or using a fact to support a predecessor fact. For example, "I know three left-handed kids who are really smart. Left-handed kids are smart. Molly is left-handed, so she must be smart."

Compound question. A question that asks two or more questions at once: "Are you going to the store or the airport?"

Conditioning a question. Responding to a question with a phrase that appears to answer it, but doesn't really. For example, "Did you have a meeting this morning?" "I got together with a couple of the guys at the office to go over some things."

Conjecture question. A question inviting imagination, such as, "What would your trip have been like if...?" It has value in determining where a subject looks while constructing a story, rather than remembering one.

Control question. A question to which you know the answer.

Displaced expectation. An expectation that relies on a set of assumptions that are no longer valid; used by interrogators and abusive spouses, for example, to keep the subject wondering, "How can I make this stop?" or "How can I please him?"

Entitlement. Something tangible or intangible to which you believe you have a right, such as fidelity, love, a clean house, respect, or use of the car every afternoon.

Filter. An internal device that interprets stimuli; filters can be sensory, cultural, religious, ethnic, physical, racial, and so on.

Leading question. A question that projects the answer in the question; for example, "How ashamed are you of running the red light?" instead of "Describe your actions at the intersection of 8th and Main Street yesterday at 11:30."

Limbic mode. The state in which emotions take over; it signifies a loss of cognitive ability.

Repeat question. The same question asked in different words; it's used as a way to determine whether the source has answered truthfully.

Shadowy memories. When the limbic system transfers information into memory in a highly emotional state, then the way a person recalls the memory could happen in unpredictable ways; a dark alley might arouse a shadowy memory of a rape, for example.

Shock of capture. A sense of being overwhelmed by the sudden, strange events related to capture; shock of capture can occur in any situation in which an individual suddenly experiences an extreme loss of control and normalcy at the hands of another. This is the ultimate in displaced expectations.

Soft interrogation. A style of interrogation credited to German interrogator Hans Scharff, who used techniques to earn prisoners' trust; it relies on understanding human behavior and psychology, rather than any type of physical cruelty.

Source lead. Information dropped by the source in the course of conversation that the questioner feels there is value in pursuing. For example, in a job interview, the candidate might say, "Thanks for having the meeting at nine" because he's in a golf tournament at noon; the interviewer might come back to that to determine whether or not golf would take precedence over work.

Stockholm Syndrome. The sense of relationship a captive feels for the captor. Whether or wittingly or unwittingly, the captor convinces the person that the only way to feel worthwhile again is be compliant, to relate to his point of view and situation.

Trailing. A fading off at the end of a sentence; this could be muttered syllables, nonsense, or simply quieter speech. Some people trail their sentences normally, but others only do it if they don't want you to hear what they're saying.

Vague question. A fuzzy question that could be simply a badly phrased question or that could be used as a diversion from the meat of the conversation; for example, "When you went to the hotel, did it seem like there were a lot of people just hanging out in the lobby?"

Index

About the Authors

G regory Hartley's expertise as an interrogator first earned him honors with the U.S. Army. More recently, it has drawn organizations such as the CIA and national TV to seek his insights about "how to" as well as "why."

Hartley has an illustrious military record, including earning the prestigious Knowlton Award, which recognizes individuals who have contributed significantly to the promotion of Army Intelligence. He graduated from the U.S. Army Interrogation School, the Anti-Terrorism Instructor Qualification Course, the Principle Protection Instructor Qualification Course, several Behavioral Symptom Analysis Seminars, and SERE (Survival, Evasion, Resistance, Escape) school. His skills as an expert interrogator earned praise while he served as SERE Instructor, Operational Interrogation Support to the 5th Special Forces Group during operation Desert Storm, Interrogation Trainer, and as a creator and director of several joint-force, multi-national interrogation exercises from 1994 to 2000. Among his military awards are the Meritorious Service Medal (which he received twice), Army Commendation Medal (of which he is a five-time recipient), Army Achievement Medal (which he received four times), National Defense Service Medal, Southwest Asia

Service Medal, and Kuwait Liberation Medal. He also attended law school at Rutgers University.

Hartley has provided expert interrogation analysis for major network and cable television, particularly Fox News, as well as National Public Radio and prime print media such as *The Washington Post* and *Philadelphia Inquirer.* Important foreign media such as *Der Spiegel* have also relied on his commentary.

Maryann Karinch is the author of seven books, including the successful business book, *Rangers Lead the Way: The Army Rangers' Guide to Leading Your Organization Through Chaos* (Adams Media, 2003). Others published works are *Dr. David Sherer's Hospital Survival Guide* (with co-author David Sherer, MD; Claren Books, 2003); *Diets Designed for Athletes* (Human Kinetics, 2001); *Empowering Underachievers: How to Guide Failing Kids (8–18) to Personal Excellence* (co-author Dr. Peter Spevak; New Horizon Press, 2000); *Lessons from the Edge: Extreme Athletes Show You How to Take on High Risk and Succeed* (Simon & Schuster, 2000); *Boot Camp: The Sergeant's Fitness and Nutrition Program* (with co-author Patrick "The Sarge" Avon; Simon & Schuster, 1999); and *Telemedicine: What the Future Holds When You're Ill* (New Horizon Press, 1994).

Earlier in her career, she managed a professional theater and raised funds for arts and education programs in Washington, D.C. She holds Bachelor's and Master's degrees in speech and drama from The Catholic University of America in Washington, D.C.